"Information through Innovation"

Contributors

The Publisher would like to express great appreciation to those individuals that contributed to the overall development of the STAR Series.

Joseph Dennin
Fairfield University

Edward Harms
Interactive Business Systems, Inc.

Philip J. Judd
Napier & Judd, Inc.

H. Albert Napier
Rice University

Kathleen M. Stewart
Moraine Valley Community College

Patrice Gapen
Laramie County Community College

Mary Z. Last
Grand Valley State University

Patricia McMahon
Moraine Valley Community College

Philip J. Pratt
Grand Valley State University

dBASE IV Version 1.1

A volume in the Boyd & Fraser STAR Series

Philip J. Pratt
Grand Valley State University

boyd & fraser publishing company

Credits:

Acquisitions Editor: James H. Edwards
Production Coordinator: Pat Stephan
Manufacturing Coordinator: Dean Sherman
Composition: Gex, Inc.
Cover Design: Hannus Design, Inc.

boyd & fraser

A Division of South-Western Publishing Company
Danvers, MA 01923

Manufactured in the United States of America.

The Star Series is printed on recycled, acid-free paper that meets Environmental Protection Agency standards.

ISBN: 0-87835-741-6

1 2 3 4 5 6 7 8 9 10 DH 5 4 3 2

Brief Table of Contents

Contents

Editor's Foreword

This book is one of many in the Boyd & Fraser *Software Training and Reference (STAR) Series*. The manuals in this Series are intended to provide an exceptionally innovative approach to learning popular application software programs, while at the same time providing a source for future reference—so that skills learned can be applied to constantly changing activities.

The overall development of the STAR Series is based upon the following principles:

- In order for any application software manual to be effective it must be organized with the outlook or orientation of a novice user in mind. A novice intuitively approaches a program from the perspective of what he or she would like "to do" or accomplish, rather than from the command perspective of experienced users. *It is for this reason that the STAR Series utilizes a user-oriented topical sequence.*

- There are common concepts underlying the various application software programs within the same general category (i. e., word processing, spreadsheet, database). If users are able to understand these common concepts, they will more likely take greater advantage of the associated program features. In addition, they will have less difficulty implementing the concepts within some different future program environment. While the "how to" of a particular program feature may change or evolve, the "why" and "when" are less likely to do so. That is, while particular application software skills are often not transferrable between programs, the underlying concepts are. *It is for this reason that each topical presentation within the STAR Series begins with a conceptual discussion.*

- There is no substitute for "learning-by-doing". Complete understanding of the concepts-skill linkage can only really be achieved through hands-on activity. *It is for this reason that each STAR Series topic presentation centers around a hands-on tutorial application, highlighting the skill(s) necessary to implement the program feature.*

- Completion of a particular example alone, however, is insufficient for understanding the various nuances of a skill. *Hence relatively extensive exercises and problems, as well as reference material applicable to generalized situations, is provided within each STAR Series manual.*

- In most other tutorial based software training manuals, the actual keystroke activities required to accomplish a tutorial are all too often lost in the surrounding explanatory material. Many users of these manuals become confused and frustrated. *It is for this reason that the STAR Series provides clear, easily distinguishable tutorial steps and directions.*

Each and every manual within the STAR Series is organized in the same consistent format. The selection of end-user-oriented topics focuses on those most fundamental to effective utilization of the program. In addition, each manual within the same general application software category is organized as similarly as possible, while still allowing for individual program variations.

Each topic begins with a conceptual discussion of the selected program features. In this **concepts section** the feature is defined, and the usefulness and applicability of the feature is presented. The conceptual discussion of the topic is followed by a complete keystroke-by-keystroke **tutorial section**. Each action step is easily identified and numerous screen images provide both useful "status checks" and reassuring positive reinforcement.

Following the tutorial section of the topic presentation is the **procedure summary section**. Procedure summaries provide not only useful review of the required implementation procedures or skills, but also serve as a general keystroke reference for applying those skills to future activities.

Throughout the topic presentation are numerous **tips** that include short items of interest, alternative methods for feature implementation, reference to associated topics, and advice on how to avoid common mistakes or overcome common difficulties. Concluding each topic is an **exercise section** for further hands-on skill development.

Each STAR Series manual is divided into three or more parts, each of which concludes with a **checkpoint**. The checkpoints contain numerous "What You Should Know" items designed to emphasize what can be accomplished within the particular program environment. The checkpoints also contain review questions and problems of intermediate difficulty, focusing on material covered up to that checkpoint. Each manual concludes with a **comprehensive problem** that integrates many of the program features within a single application.

DOS Coverage

In order to keep the overall length (and price) of each STAR Series manual down to a reasonable level, and to avoid the possibly unnecessary repitition of fundamental DOS concepts and skills, it was decided to provide DOS coverage separately through a single stand-alone book. Such DOS operating system coverage may be obtained through *DOS Essentials*, by Rod B. Southworth, an inexpensive sixty-four page booklet also published by Boyd & Fraser.

Instructor's Materials

A comprehensive Instructor's Manual is available for use in conjunction with each STAR Series offering. The Instructor's Manual contains topic overviews, key terms, lecture notes, software suggestions, solutions to all exercises and problems, answers to checkpoint review questions, additional comprehensive exercises and solutions, and over 250 test questions. Also available is an Instructor's Resource Disk containing tutorial, exercise, and problem files in various stages of completion.

Series Philosophy — Diversity and Currency

Boyd & Fraser intends to extend the STAR Series to include coverage of all popular application software programs. In addition, we are committed to providing timely coverage of all program updates and revisions. It is hoped that the consistent STAR Series organization and format will provide a flexible approach to either learning multiple application programs or updating to newer program versions. Please contact your local South-Western/Boyd & Fraser Representative for information on current and future STAR Series offerings.

Introduction to Databases

Creating, storing, sorting, and retrieving data are important tasks faced by individuals living in a complex society. In our personal lives, most of us maintain a variety of records such as the names, addresses, and telephone numbers of friends and business associates; records of investments; and records of expenses for income tax purposes. Not only must these types of records be maintained, but the records must be arranged so that the data within each record can be easily accessed when required. In the business world, maintaining information that can be quickly and easily accessed is crucial to success. Employee personnel records must be maintained, inventory records kept, and payroll information and other types of data must be accumulated and periodically updated.

We use the term **database** to describe a collection of data organized in a manner that allows access, retrieval, and use of that data. The basic idea of a database is quite simple. It is a structure that can hold data concerning many different types of objects (technically called **entities**) as well as the relationships among these objects. For example, a database for a company might hold data on such objects as sales reps and customers. In addition, the database would include the relationship between sales reps and customers. For example, using the data in the database, we must be able to determine which sales rep represents a particular customer as well as which customers are represented by a given sales rep.

Figure 1 gives a sample of such a database. Note that it consists of two tables: SLSREP and CUSTOMER. The columns in the SLSREP table include the sales rep number, name, address, total commission, and commission rate. Thus the name of sales rep 3 is Mary Jones. She lives at 123 Main St. in Grant, Michigan. Her total commission is $2150.00, and her commission rate is 5 percent.

The first five columns in the CUSTOMER table include the customer number, name, address, current balance, and credit limit. Thus the name of customer 622 is Dan Martin. He lives at 419 Chip St. in Grant, Michigan. His current balance is $575.50, which happens to exceed his $500 credit limit.

Figure 1

Sales Rep and Customer Tables

SLSREP

SLSREP_ NUMBER	SLSREP_NAME	SLSREP_ADDRESS	TOTAL_ COMMISSION	COMMISSION_ RATE
3	MARY JONES	123 MAIN,GRANT,MI	2150.00	05
6	WILLIAM SMITH	102 RAYMOND,ADA,MI	4912.50	07
12	SAM BROWN	419 HARPER,LANSING,MI	2150.00	05

CUSTOMER

CUSTOMER_ NUMBER	NAME	ADDRESS	CURRENT_ BALANCE	CREDIT_ LIMIT	SLSREP_ NUMBER
124	SALLY ADAMS	481 OAK,LANSING,MI	418.75	500	3
256	ANN SAMUELS	215 PETE,GRANT,MI	10.75	800	6
311	DON CHARLE	48 COLLEGE,IRA,MI	200.10	300	12
315	TOM DANIELS	914 CHERRY,KENT,MI	320.75	300	6
405	AL WILLIAMS	519 WATSON,GRANT,MI	201.75	800	12
412	SUSAN LIN	16 ELM,LANSING,MI	908.75	1000	3
522	MARY NELSON	108 PINE,ADA,MI	49.50	800	12
567	JOE BAKER	808 RIDGE,HARPER,MI	201.20	300	6
587	JUDY ROBERTS	512 PINE,ADA,MI	57.75	500	6
622	DAN MARTIN	419 CHIP,GRANT,MI	575.50	500	3

The last column in the CUSTOMER table serves a very special purpose. It relates customers and sales reps. Using this column, we can see that Dan Martin's sales rep is sales rep 3 (Mary Jones). Likewise, we can see that Mary Jones represents customers 124 (Sally Adams), 412 (Susan Lin), and 622 (Dan Martin). We do this by first looking up Mary's number in the SLSREP table and then looking for all the rows in the CUSTOMER table that contain this number in the column labeled SLSREP_NUMBER.

In a very real sense, the tables shown in Figure 1 form a database even if they were simply kept on paper. To obtain maximum benefit and flexibility from this database, however, the database should be kept on a computer. Then, all we would need is a tool to help users access this database. The term "database management system" describes such a tool. A **database management system**, or **DBMS**, is a software product with which users can easily create a database; make additions, deletions, and changes to data in the database; sort the data in the database; and retrieve data from the database in a variety of ways.

One very popular DBMS available for personal computers is dBASE IV. dBASE IV was developed by Ashton-Tate as a powerful DBMS, yet its commands allow users to easily create and manage the databases they need for either personal or business use. dBASE IV is one of a general category of database management systems called **relational.** In simplest terms, this means that we can visualize the data in the database exactly as we saw earlier, that is, as a collection of tables, each consisting of a series of rows and columns.

Note From this point on dBASE IV is referred to simply as dBASE.

Before we proceed, you should be aware of the following information concerning working with dBASE:

1. In general, filenames can contain a three-character extension (the characters following the period in the name of the file). dBASE has its own extensions that it adds to filenames. This is nothing for you to worry about. You just indicate the regular part of the name, and dBASE does the rest automatically. On some screens you will see these extensions, but you do not need to do anything with them.
2. The NumLock key on your keyboard switches your keyboard in and out of NumLock mode. In NumLock mode, you can use the numeric keypad on your keyboard to enter numbers. If you are not in NumLock mode, you use the keypad for cursor movement. (If your keyboard does not have separate cursor movement keys, you do not want to be in NumLock mode. If you have separate cursor movement keys, you might very well decide to be in NumLock mode. It's up to you.) If you are in NumLock mode, the letters "Num" appear on some screens. The screens shown in the text include these letters. If you are not in NumLock mode, your screens do not include these letters. This is not a problem. Just be aware of this slight difference between what appears on your screen and what is shown in the text.
3. Most relational database management systems use the terms **table**, **row**, and **column.** dBASE, however, uses the terms **database file**, **record**, and **field**. As you read through the dBASE material, be aware of this difference. The correspondence between the two sets of terms is as follows:

General Term	dBASE Term
table	database file
row	record
column	field

We use the employee records shown in Figure 2 in our sample database. Each record contains an employee number, the employee's name, the data hired, a department name, the employee's pay rate, and an entry indicating whether the employee is a member of the union. The rows in this table are the records. The columns are the fields. The whole table is a database file.

Figure 2
Employee Table

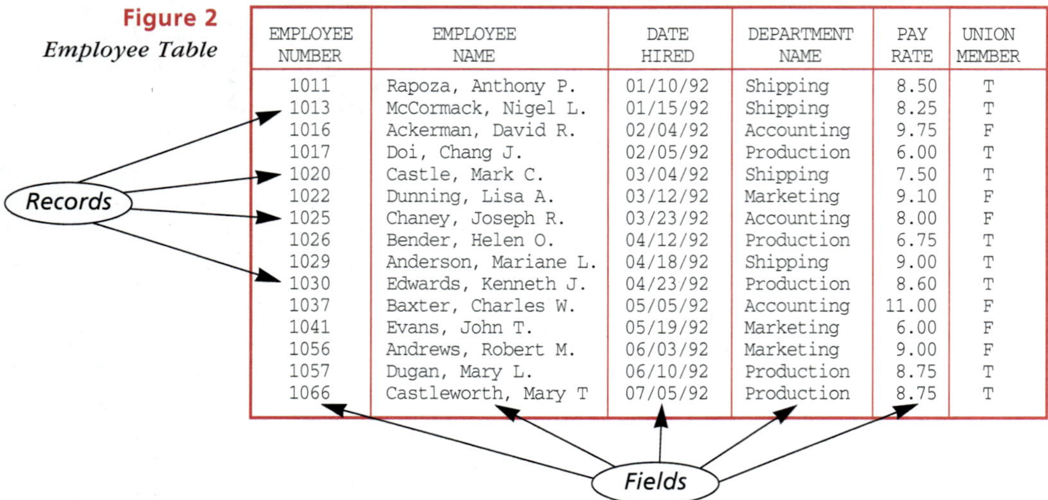

EMPLOYEE NUMBER	EMPLOYEE NAME	DATE HIRED	DEPARTMENT NAME	PAY RATE	UNION MEMBER
1011	Rapoza, Anthony P.	01/10/92	Shipping	8.50	T
1013	McCormack, Nigel L.	01/15/92	Shipping	8.25	T
1016	Ackerman, David R.	02/04/92	Accounting	9.75	F
1017	Doi, Chang J.	02/05/92	Production	6.00	T
1020	Castle, Mark C.	03/04/92	Shipping	7.50	T
1022	Dunning, Lisa A.	03/12/92	Marketing	9.10	F
1025	Chaney, Joseph R.	03/23/92	Accounting	8.00	F
1026	Bender, Helen O.	04/12/92	Production	6.75	T
1029	Anderson, Mariane L.	04/18/92	Shipping	9.00	T
1030	Edwards, Kenneth J.	04/23/92	Production	8.60	T
1037	Baxter, Charles W.	05/05/92	Accounting	11.00	F
1041	Evans, John T.	05/19/92	Marketing	6.00	F
1056	Andrews, Robert M.	06/03/92	Marketing	9.00	F
1057	Dugan, Mary L.	06/10/92	Production	8.75	T
1066	Castleworth, Mary T	07/05/92	Production	8.75	T

Using dBASE

CONCEPTS

To use dBASE, you must first load the computer's operating system. Then you can load dBASE into the computer's main memory.

Loading dBASE

11

The actual method you use to load dBASE depends on your particular computer. Instructions for loading dBASE from the system prompt are given in both the tutorial and procedure summary sections of this topic.

Once you have loaded dBASE, your display should look like the one shown in Figure 1.1. This is called the **Control Center**. It is the screen from which you begin most of your work. Let's look at the various portions of the Control Center.

The area at the top of the screen where you see the words "Catalog," "Tools," and "Exit" is called the menu bar. Each of the three terms (Catalog, Tools, and Exit) represents a menu. A **menu** is simply a list of actions from which you can choose. As you work with dBASE, the words listed at the top of the screen may change, but the list itself always plays the same role. It is a collection of menus that you access to select the action you wish to take next.

Farther down the screen is a line that begins with CATALOG:. A **catalog** is simply a collection of related files. It is like a file folder that helps you organize your paperwork. You will have a chance to create and use catalogs throughout this text. The various files you create will be grouped into these catalogs.

Figure 1.1
Control Center

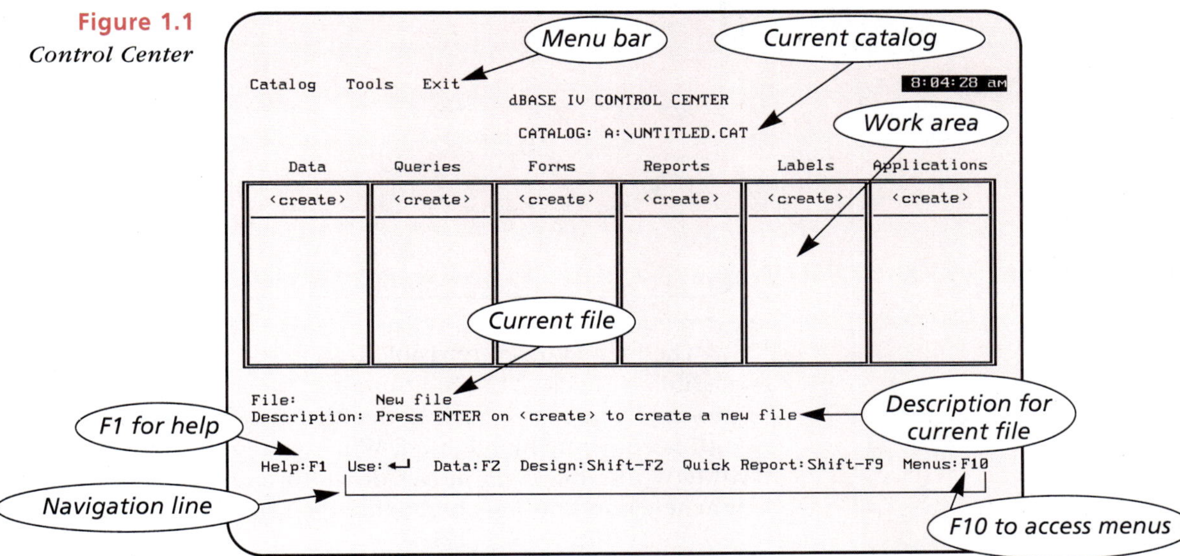

The CATALOG line on the screen indicates which catalog is currently in use. In the figure it indicates that a special catalog, called UNTITLED, is in use. You will learn how to switch from one catalog to another and what happens when you do.

The big box on the screen is called the **work area**. It lists the various types of files that are in the current catalog. One of these files or the word <create> is highlighted. The highlighted file appears after the word "File," and a description of it appears after the word "Description." If <create> is highlighted, the filename and description appear as shown in Figure 1.1.

The line at the bottom of the screen is called the **navigation line**. It tells you how some special keys function. The navigation line in Figure 1.1, for example, shows that you can press function key 1 (the key labeled F1 on your keyboard) to obtain help or press F10 to use the menus.

All of this detail may seem confusing at first. Once you master a few simple rules, however, you will be able to work your way through the various steps without much difficulty.

Selecting an Option 11

To select an option from a menu, you first press F10. You are now in Menu mode (Figure 1.2), where you indicate the option you wish to select by picking it from a menu. (Don't worry about the meaning of the specific choices for now.)

Figure 1.2
Catalog Menu

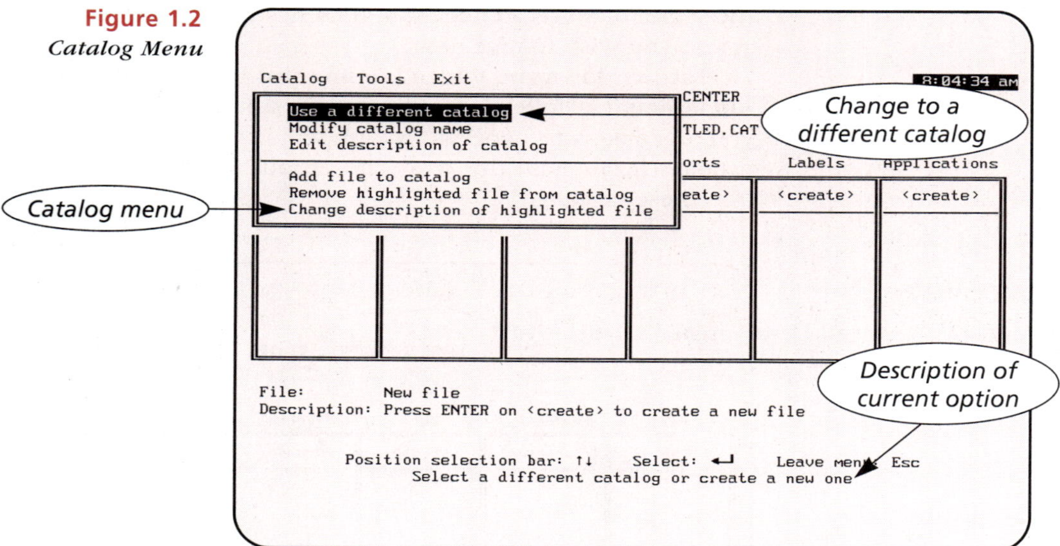

The menu currently visible on the screen is the Catalog menu. The possible choices—"Use a different catalog," "Modify catalog name," and so on—are listed in the box. Notice that the first choice, "Use a different catalog," is currently highlighted. When you repeatedly press the DOWN ARROW, the highlight moves down through some of the other choices. Whenever an option is highlighted, a brief description of the option appears at the bottom of the screen, under the navigation line. Depending on what actions you have taken before you pressed F10, some of these options may not be currently available to you. The highlight automatically skips over such options.

Pressing the RIGHT ARROW moves you to the next menu on the list, in this case the Tools menu. Pressing the LEFT ARROW key moves you to the previous menu.

To recap, you bring the menus to the screen by pressing F10. You move from one menu to another by using the LEFT and RIGHT ARROW keys. Within a menu, you move from one option to another by using the UP and DOWN ARROW keys.

The final step in the process is to actually make the selection. To do so, make sure the option you wish to select is highlighted by using the appropriate arrow keys and then press ENTER.

Moving from Dot Prompt to Control Center 12

Besides using the Control Center, you can also use the **dot prompt** in dBASE. The only reason we mention it here is so that if you inadvertently switch to this mode, you will recognize it and be able to return to the Control Center. For example, when you want to exit dBASE, you should pick the "Quit to DOS" option of the Exit menu (Figure 1.3). If you select "Exit to dot prompt" by mistake, you will find yourself in **Dot Prompt mode** and your screen should look like Figure 1.4. Notice the single dot near the lower corner of the screen. This is the dot prompt.

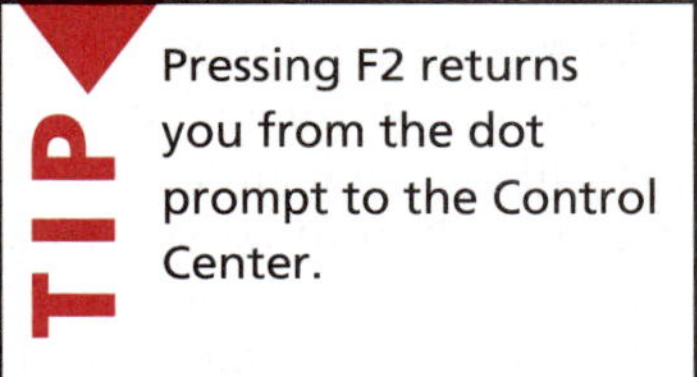

TIP
Pressing F2 returns you from the dot prompt to the Control Center.

Fortunately, if you ever find yourself at the dot prompt, you can easily return to the Control Center. Simply press F2 and the Control Center appears once again on your screen.

Figure 1.3
Exit Menu

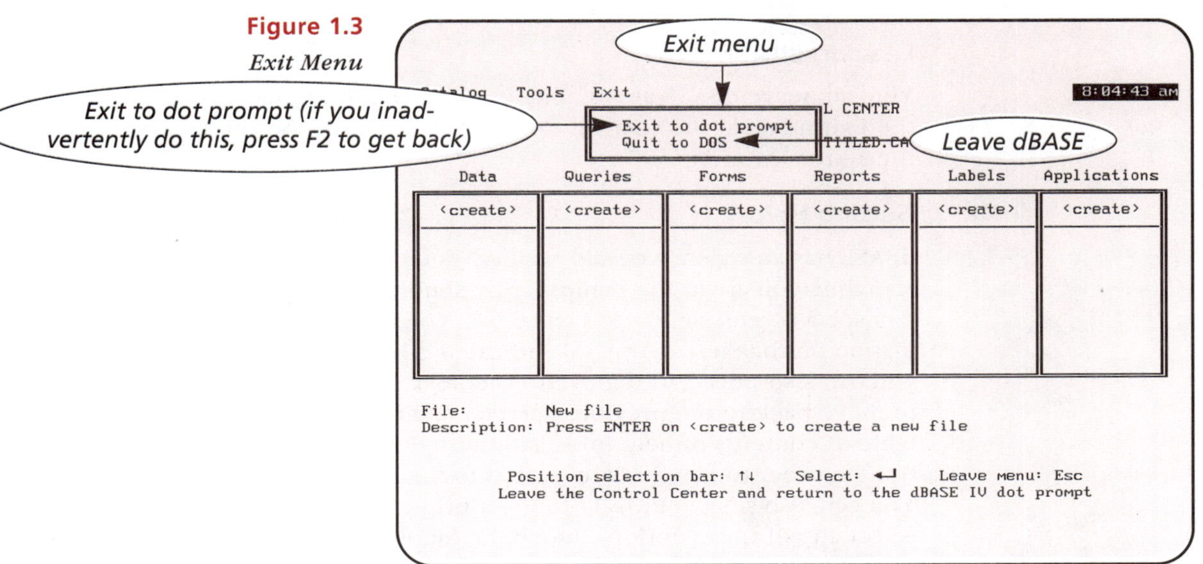

Figure 1.4

Dot Prompt Screen

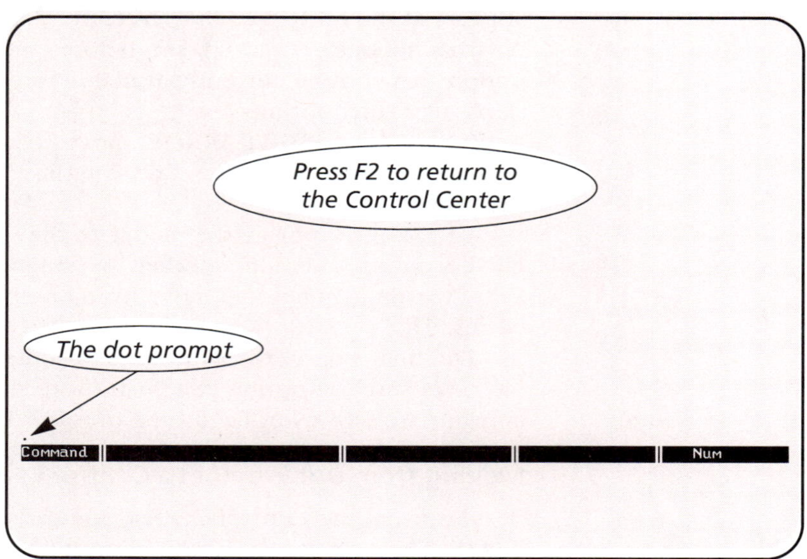

Escaping from an Operation (12)

Sometimes you might find that you unintentionally chose the wrong option. In other cases, you might not want to proceed with some action you have started, but you are not sure how to get out. In such situations, simply press the ESCAPE key. Sometimes this immediately returns you to the Control Center. Other times, you may first be asked whether or not you really want to escape from the task on which you are working. In still others, you may need to press ESCAPE more than once to return to the Control Center.

Leaving dBASE (12)

You can leave dBASE at any time by selecting the "Quit to DOS" option of the Exit menu at the Control Center. Selecting this option returns you to the system prompt.

Getting Help (12)

dBASE has an extensive Help facility. You can get help on a variety of topics while you are at the computer by simply pressing F1. When you do, you see a screen similar to Figure 1.5. You may only need to read the information on that screen, but, as indicated on the bottom line of this screen, you can also press F4 to move to the next screen of help information or F3 to move back to the previous screen. You can select "CONTENTS" to see a table of contents of help information or "RELATED TOPICS" to get information on other topics that are related to the topic you are currently viewing. You can also select "PRINT" to get a printed copy of the information. To select any of these options, move the highlight to the one you want and press ENTER. When you have finished looking, press ESCAPE.

Figure 1.5

Help Screen

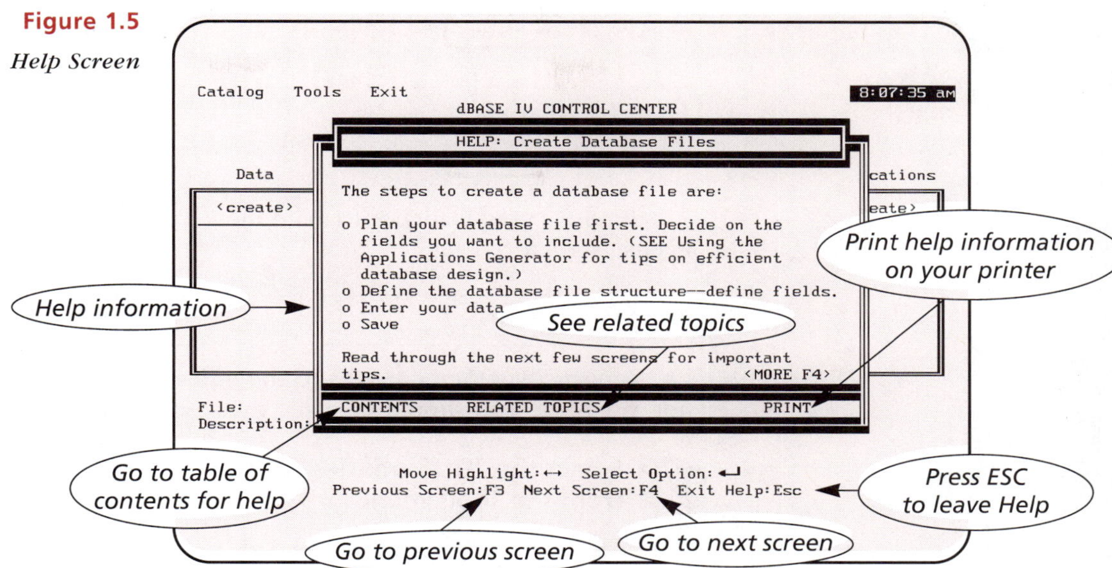

When you request help, you get information that relates to the task on which you are working. If, for example, you have highlighted a particular menu option, the information will concern that menu option. However, you can use the table of contents to obtain help on any topic.

TUTORIAL In this tutorial, you become familiar with the basic way to use dBASE. You begin by starting dBASE. (The way in which you do so depends on your particular computer. Check with your instructor to make sure the following steps are appropriate in your specific situation.)

1 **Start dBASE.** Place your data disk in drive A.

Type	a:	in either upper- or lowercase.
Press	 ENTER	Makes drive A the default drive.

> **TIP** If dBASE has been installed in the usual manner, the required path command is executed automatically when you boot your computer. In that case, you can skip this step. Check with your instructor to see if this is the case.

The next command creates the required path to the directory containing dBASE.

Type	path C:\dbase	Creates required path to directory containing dBASE.

This command assumes that dBASE is located in a directory called dbase on drive C. ◀

Press	↵ ENTER	Makes directory containing dBASE the default directory.
Type	dbase	in either upper- or lowercase.
Press	↵ ENTER	

dBASE is now loaded into main memory, and you will see the dBASE license screen.

Press	↵ ENTER	or wait a few seconds.

Your display then changes to the one shown in Figure 1.1. If it does not, press F2. You should then see the screen shown in Figure 1.1.

2 Select the "DOS utilities" option from the Tools menu.

Press	F10	Moves to Menu mode.
Press	→	Moves to Tools menu.
Press	↓ three times	Moves to "DOS utilities" option.
Press	↵ ENTER	

3 Escape from the operation you have begun.

Press	ESC	You are now asked if you wish to abandon the operation.
Press	←	Moves to "Yes."
Press	↵ ENTER	

You should see the main Control Center screen.

4 Move to the dot prompt.

Select	"Exit to dot prompt"	from the Exit menu.

5 Return from the dot prompt to the Control Center.

Press	F2	

You should see the main Control Center screen.

6 **Leave dBASE.**

Select	"Quit to DOS"	from Exit menu.

7 **Restart dBASE.** Follow the instructions given in Task 1.

8 **Get help on the "DOS utilities" option from the Tools menu.**

Press	F10	Moves to Menu mode.
Press	→	Moves to Tools menu.
Press	↓ three times	Moves to "DOS utilities" option.
Press	F1	Gets help information.
Press	ESC	Removes help information from screen.
Press	ESC	Returns to Control Center.

PROCEDURE SUMMARY

LOADING dBASE

Place your data disk in drive A.	
Enter the drive designation where your data disk is located.	a: ↵ENTER
If the correct path has not been set up already (see your instructor to check whether or not this is the case), type path c:\dbase.	path C:\dbase ↵ENTER
Start dBASE.	dbase ↵ENTER

SELECTING AN OPTION

Move to menus.	F10
Move to the desired menu.	← or →
Move the highlight to the desired option.	↑ or ↓
Make the selection.	↵ENTER

MOVING FROM DOT PROMPT TO CONTROL CENTER	Move to the Control Center.	F2
ESCAPING FROM AN OPERATION	Abandon the operation.	ESC
	If you are asked if you want to abandon the operation, answer "Yes."	←, ↵ ENTER
LEAVING dBASE	Select the "Quit to DOS" option of the Exit menu at the Control Center.	
GETTING HELP	Get Help.	F1
	Once you have viewed the information, leave Help.	ESC

EXERCISES

1. Load dBASE into main memory.
2. Select the "Export" option of the Tools menu.
3. Escape from the operation you have begun.
4. Leave dBASE.
5. Restart dBASE.
6. Move to the dot prompt.
7. Move back to the Control Center.
8. Get help on the "Export" option of the Tools menu.

Creating a Database File

CONCEPTS Before you can use a database file, you must create it. To do so, you must describe the structure of the file to dBASE; that is, you must describe the fields that make up the database and indicate the characteristics of these fields.

Creating a Catalog 18

A **catalog** is a collection of related files. When a database file (as well as the other types of files you will create later) is created, it is placed in the catalog that is currently active. Thus, before you create a database file, you must make sure that the catalog into which it is to be placed is active. If the desired catalog does not yet exist, you must create it. You can create or activate a catalog with the same option, the "Use a different catalog" option of the Catalog menu. Once you have created a new catalog or activated an existing one, the files you create are automatically placed in this catalog.

Creating a Database File

You must assign the database file a name. The rules for database filenames are as follows:

1. The name can be up to eight characters long.
2. The first character must be a letter of the alphabet.
3. The remaining characters can be letters, numeric digits, or the underscore (_).
4. No blank spaces are allowed.

You use the Database Design screen (Figure 2.1) to describe the fields in your database file. On this screen, you enter the information on all the fields in the database file. The status line shows that:

1. You are creating a database file.
2. The default drive is A: (yours might be different).
3. You are creating a new file. (If you were working on a file that already existed, its name would appear in the spot currently occupied by <NEW>.)
4. You are currently working on the first field.
5. So far there is only this one field.

Figure 2.1
Database Design Screen

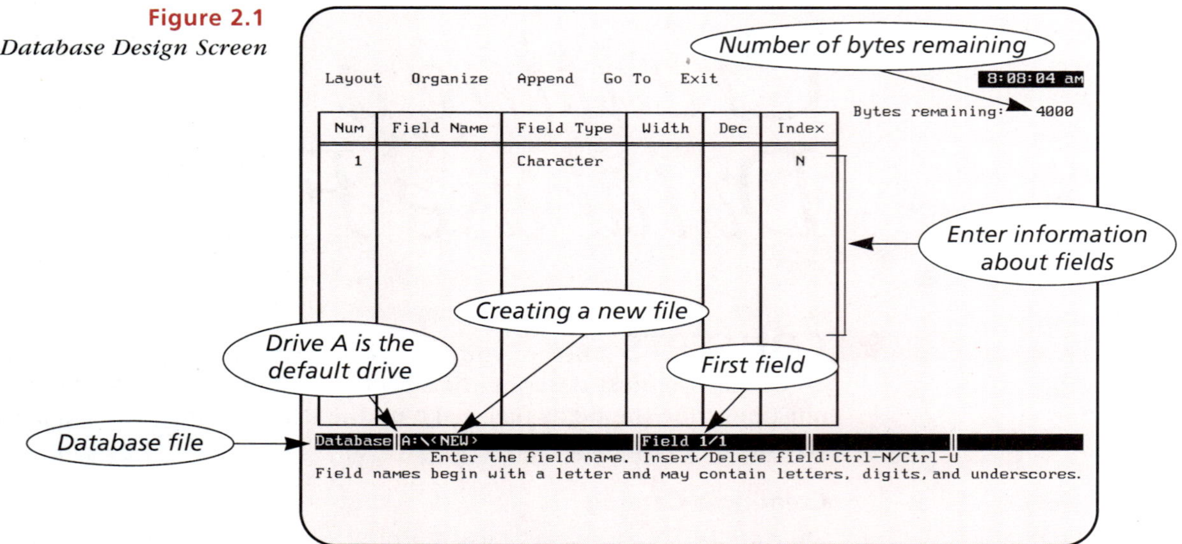

To define the structure of the database file, you must specify the following information for each field:

1. **Field Name.** Each field in a database file must be given a unique name. The name should be descriptive of the contents of the field. The first character of the name must be alphabetic. The remaining characters can consist of letters of the alphabet, numerical digits, or the underscore (_). No blank spaces are allowed within the field name.

2. **Field Type.** For each field, you must also indicate the field type, that is, the type of data that the field will contain. The available field types are:

   CHARACTER fields—may be used to store any printable character that can be entered from the keyboard. This includes letters of the alphabet, numbers, special characters, and blanks. A maximum of 254 characters may be included in a CHARACTER field.

   DATE fields—are used to store dates. Unless otherwise specified, dates are stored in the form of MM/DD/YY (month/day/year). The width of the DATE field is always eight characters.

   NUMERIC fields—are used to store integer numbers or decimal numbers. Integer numbers are numbers that do not contain a decimal point. NUMERIC fields may contain a plus (+) or minus (-) sign. Accuracy is to 15 digits. A field must be defined as numeric if the field is to be used in an arithmetic calculation.

   LOGICAL fields—consist of a single value representing a true or false condition. The entry must consist of T (True), F (False), Y (Yes), or N (No). The width of the LOGICAL field is always one character.

   MEMO fields—are used to store large blocks of text such as words or sentences. MEMO fields may be up to 4000 characters long.

3. **Field Width.** For each field, you must also type the width. The width of the field indicates the maximum number of characters that the field will contain. (The decimal position specifies the location of the decimal point. For example, a decimal position of 2 indicates that there are two positions to the right of the decimal point.)
4. **Decimal Places.** For NUMERIC fields, you must also enter the number of decimal places, that is, the number of positions to the right of the decimal point.
5. **Index.** You must indicate whether or not dBASE is to maintain an index for the field. (You will learn about indexes later. For now, just make the entries as indicated in the text for indexes.)

You should know two special things about entering this information:

1. If you type an entry that completely fills the space available for it on the screen, the cursor automatically advances to the next position. If your entry does not fill the available space, you must press ENTER to advance the cursor.
2. When you enter the field type, all you need to do is repeatedly press the spacebar until the type you want is displayed and then press ENTER.

If you discover that you have made a mistake in creating your database file after you have returned to the Control Center, you can correct the structure of your database in two ways. If you have not added any records to the file, you can start over by selecting the "Quit to DOS" option of the Exit menu of the Control Center to return to DOS and using the Erase command to erase your database file. In the Erase command, you need to give the full name of your database file as well as the drive. To erase the EMPLOYEE database file in drive A, the command would be ERASE A:EMPLOYEE.DBF. Once you have erased the file, you can start dBASE and begin the process from scratch. If you do not discover the mistake until after you have added all the data, you must modify the structure of your database. (See details in Topic 18.)

TUTORIAL

In this tutorial, you first create the EMPCAT catalog. Then you create the EMPLOYEE database file by describing the fields within it to dBASE. Figure 2.2 gives the field names that are used in this database file as well as the characteristics of the fields.

1 Create the EMPCAT catalog.

Select	"Use a different catalog"	from Catalog menu.
Select	<create>	Creates new catalog.
Type	EMPCAT	Names new catalog.
Press	↵ ENTER	

Figure 2.2
Field Names and Characteristics for Employee File

FIELD DESCRIPTION	FIELD NAME	FIELD TYPE	WIDTH	DECIMAL POSITIONS	INDEX
EMPLOYEE NUMBER	NUMBER	CHARACTER	4		Y
EMPLOYEE NAME	NAME	CHARACTER	20		N
DATE HIRED	DATE	DATE	8		N
DEPARTMENT NAME	DEPARTMENT	CHARACTER	10		N
PAY RATE	PAY_RATE	NUMERIC	5	2	N
UNION MEMBER	UNION	LOGICAL	1		N

Decimal positions only necessary for numeric fields

The catalog you created, EMPCAT, is now the active catalog.

2 Create the EMPLOYEE database file.

Select	<create>	in Data column.

You are now taken to the screen used to design a database (Figure 2.1).

Type	NUMBER
Press	↵ ENTER twice

The correct field type is already displayed.

Type	4
Press	↵ ENTER
Type	Y

There will be an index. Make the entries for the second field.

Type	NAME
Press	↵ ENTER twice
Type	20
Press	↵ ENTER
Type	N

There will not be an index. Make the remaining entries as shown in Figure 2.3. To specify DATE as a field type, press the spacebar until the word "Date" appears in the Field Type column. dBASE then automatically specifies the width as 8. (The slashes in a date count as positions in the field.) To specify LOGICAL as a field type, press the spacebar until the word "Logical" appears in the Field Type column. dBASE then automatically specifies the width as 1. Because the name DEPARTMENT occupies all positions in the field name portion of the display, when you type the last character (the ending T in DEPARTMENT), a beep sounds and the cursor automatically advances to the next column.

TIP If you make a mistake in any of these entries, use the keys shown in Table 2.1 to go back and correct it. (SHIFT-TAB means hold the SHIFT key down and press the TAB key. CTRL-N means hold the CTRL key down and type the letter N.)

Table 2.1
Special Keys Used When Designing a Database

KEY	PURPOSE
↑	Moves the highlight up one row.
↓	Moves the highlight down one row.
→	Moves the cursor one position to the right.
←	Moves the cursor one position to the left.
TAB	Moves the cursor one column to the right.
SHIFT - TAB	Moves the cursor one column to the left.
←BACKSPACE	Moves cursor one position to the left and erases character that was in that position.
↵ENTER	Completes current entry and moves cursor to the next column. If you are in the last column in a row, moves to the first column in the next row.
CTRL - N	Inserts a blank row at current cursor position.
CTRL - U	Deletes row at current cursor position.

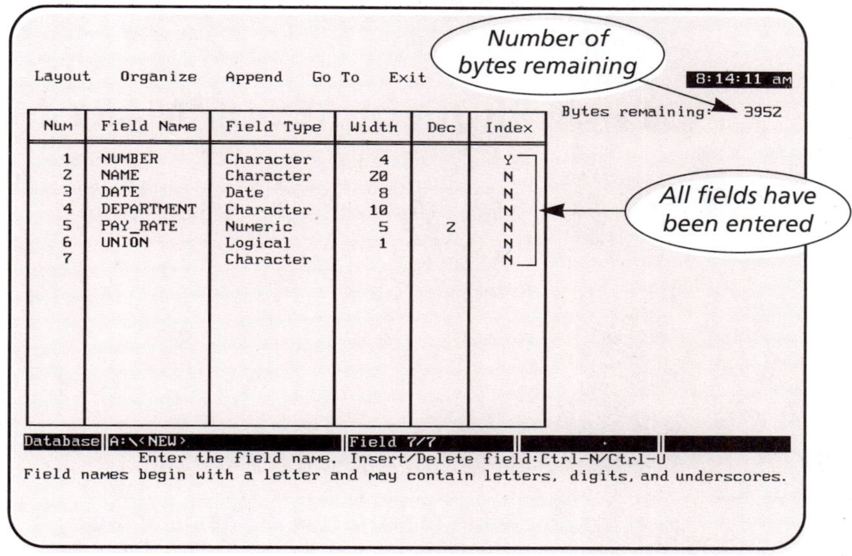

Figure 2.3
Database Design Screen

When you have made all the entries, you will have defined all the fields in the database. You now indicate to dBASE that you are done.

Select	"Save changes and exit"	from Exit menu.
Type	EMPLOYEE	Names database file.

You should now be back at the Control Center. The final step is to enter a description of this EMPLOYEE file. This is not required, but it will help you differentiate between files later.

Select	"Change description of highlighted file"	from Catalog menu.
Type	Employee database file	Gives description for file.

Note that the description you just entered appears on the screen and that the word "EMPLOYEE" appears *above* the line in the Data column. This indicates that the file is currently active. If it were not active, "EMPLOYEE" would be below the line.

When you have finished the process, feel free to leave dBASE. To do so, select the "Quit to DOS" option of the Exit menu of the Control Center. When you are ready to resume your work, start dBASE in precisely the same manner you did earlier.

PROCEDURE SUMMARY

CREATING A CATALOG

Select "Use a different catalog" from the Catalog menu.	
Select <create>.	
Enter the name of the catalog.	(your input) ↵ENTER

CREATING A DATABASE FILE

Select <create> in the Data column.	
Define the structure of the database by specifying the fields.	(your input)
Select the "Save changes and exit" option of the Exit menu.	
Enter the name of the database file.	(your input) ↵ENTER

EXERCISES

A database file is to be designed and created to store a list of personal checks and related information. The field characteristics are illustrated in the following table:

FIELD DESCRIPTION	FIELD NAME	FIELD TYPE	WIDTH	DECIMAL POSITIONS	INDEX
CHECK NUMBER	CHECKNUM	CHARACTER	4		Y
DATE	DATE	DATE	8		N
PAYEE	PAYEE	CHARACTER	18		N
CHECK AMOUNT	AMOUNT	NUMERIC	6	2	N
EXPENSE	EXPENSE	CHARACTER	14		N
TAX DEDUCTIBLE	TAXDED	LOGICAL	14		N

Perform the following tasks:

1. Insert your data disk into drive A, and then load dBASE.
2. Create a catalog called CHECKCAT.
3. Create the database file, and name it CHECK.
4. Enter the six fields in the preceding table.

Loading a Database

CONCEPTS Once you have created your database file, you are ready to load it, that is, to add records to it. To add records, the database file must be active.

> **TIP** It is a common mistake to forget to activate a database file. If you find you cannot take a particular action, verify that you activated your database file. It is active if its name appears above the line in the Data column. If no name appears, be sure to activate the database file so you can continue.

Activating a Catalog 28

Before you access data in a particular database, you first need to make sure that the catalog for that database is active. To activate a catalog, you use the "Use a different catalog" option of the Catalog menu.

Activating a Database File 28

To use a database file in dBASE, it *must* be active. You activate database files from the Control Center. Once you have activated a file, it appears above the line in the Data column. ◀

Adding Records to a Database File 28

Once you have created and activated the database file, you are ready to add records to it. With the database file active, you can use the Edit screen (Figure 3.1) to add the records. Table 3.1 describes the use of various keys you can use during the data entry process.

Figure 3.1
Edit Screen

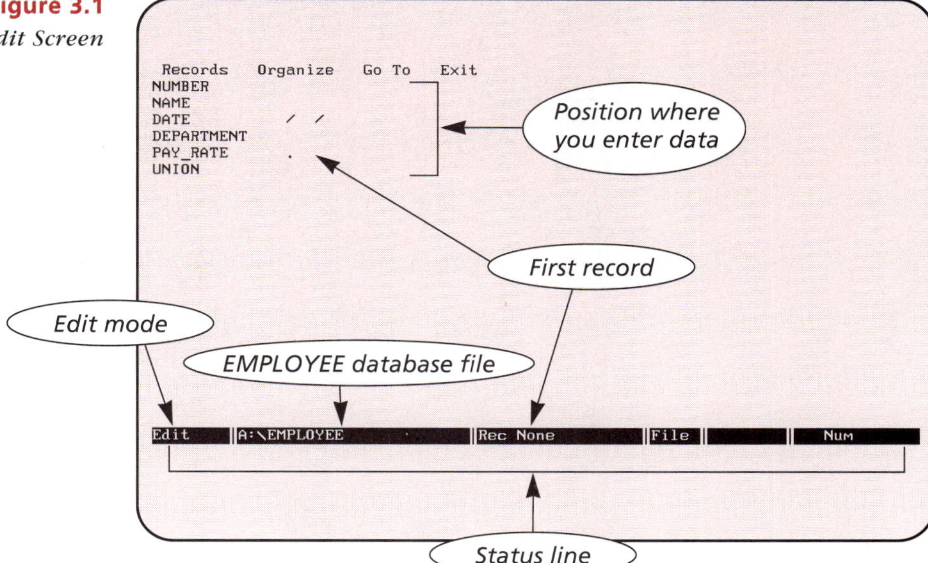

You enter the data one field at a time. The cursor automatically moves to the next line if the data entered occupies the entire width of the field. If the data does not fill the field, you must press ENTER after you have entered the data for that field. When you have finished entering the data for one record, dBASE automatically saves the record. It also clears out the data in preparation for the next record. As soon as you have completely entered the data for a record, the record is saved. Thus there is no need for a special "Save" step as you often encounter in using word processors or spreadsheet programs.

Table 3.1
Special Keys Used When Entering Data

KEY	PURPOSE
↑	Moves cursor up one row.
↓	Moves cursor down one row.
→	Moves cursor one position to right.
←	Moves cursor one position to left.
TAB	Moves to next field.
SHIFT-TAB	Moves to previous field.
PAGE DOWN	Moves to next record if you are on Edit screen. Moves down one screenful if you are on Browse screen.
PAGE UP	Moves to previous record if you are on Edit screen. Moves up one screenful if you are on Browse screen.
HOME	Moves to beginning of field if you are on Edit screen. Moves to first field in record if you are on Browse screen.
END	Moves to end of field if you are on Edit screen. Moves to last field in record if you are on Browse screen.
←BACKSPACE	Moves cursor one position to left and erases character that was in that position.
DELETE	Deletes character at current cursor position.
↵ ENTER	Completes current entry and moves cursor to next field.
CTRL-Y	Deletes all characters to right of cursor.
F2	Changes between Edit and Browse screens.
ESC	Leaves current record without saving changes.
INSERT	Switches between Insert mode and Replace mode. If in Insert mode, "Ins" displays on status line.

When you enter data, keep in mind the following points concerning two special types of fields:

1. A DATE field contains slashes. When typing a date, type a two-digit month, a two-digit day, and a two-digit year. The date will be positioned correctly around the slashes.
2. A LOGICAL field (like UNION) contains a question. When entering a value for a LOGICAL field, it is a good idea to restrict yourself to just entering T (for true) or F (for false) even though dBASE allows you to enter Y (for yes) or N (for no). It is easy to get confused if you use T or F some of the time and Y or N at other times. Further, when dBASE displays this data, it displays T or F. Thus, if you enter the letter Y, it is displayed as a T. If you enter N, it is displayed as an F. For these reasons, it makes sense to only use T or F.

Once you have some records in your database file, the F2 key possesses an interesting property. If you press F2 at the Edit screen, you move to a different screen, the Browse screen. (We'll look at the Browse screen later.) Press F2 again and you move back to the Edit screen. If you keep pressing F2, you flip back and forth between these two screens. All you really need to know about this property of F2 is that if you press F2 from the Control Center or any other screen and you end up at the wrong screen, simply press F2 a second time.

Changing Records in a Database File 28

Not only do you need to be able to add new records, you must also be able to make changes to existing records. To change existing records, the database file must be active. When it is active, you can use the same Edit screen you did to add records.

To correct a particular record, it must be on the screen. If it is not, you can use PAGE UP and PAGE DOWN to bring the desired record to the screen. Pressing PAGE UP moves you to the previous record, and pressing PAGE DOWN moves you to the next record. Press PAGE UP or PAGE DOWN enough times to bring the record you want to the screen so that you can make the necessary corrections.

Deleting Records from a Database File 29

You will occasionally find that you have records in your database file that should no longer be there. In some cases, they are simply mistakes; you typed the wrong record. In others, the records belonged there at one time, but they do not belong in the file any longer. Perhaps, for example, an employee is no longer with the company, so his or her record should no longer be in the EMPLOYEE file. In such cases, you need to be able to *delete* (remove) these records. You can delete a record by using the Edit screen, bringing the record to the screen, and pressing CONTROL-U.

When you delete a record, dBASE does not actually remove the record from the database file. Instead, it merely marks the record as being "deleted." You can see evidence of this by looking near the lower right-hand corner of your screen. You should see the letters "Del." This indicates that

> **TIP** The Organize menu can be found on the Edit screen, the Browse screen, and the Database Design screen. You can use whichever of these screens you find most convenient. The effect is the same.

the record has been so marked. Such a record can be unmarked by pressing CONTROL-U a second time. To permanently remove these marked records, you use the "Erase marked records" option of the Organize menu. When the records are permanently removed, you can no longer unmark them.

Listing Records in a Database File

29

After you have created your database file and added the necessary data to it, you need to be able to list the records and fields in the file. For example, after you have added the records to the EMPLOYEE file, you would like to list the records in it in order to make sure you have entered them correctly. dBASE provides a special option called "Quick Report" that is designed for this specific purpose.

TUTORIAL

In this tutorial, you load the EMPLOYEE database file; that is, you add data to it.

1 **Activate the EMPCAT catalog and the EMPLOYEE database file.** Check to see if "EMPCAT" appears after "CATALOG" near the top of the Control Center. If it does not, you need to activate the catalog.

Select	"Use a different catalog"	from Catalog menu.
Select	EMPCAT	from list of catalogs.

Check to see if "EMPLOYEE" appears above the line in the Data column. If it does not, you need to activate the database file.

Select	EMPLOYEE	
Select	"Use file"	Activates file.

2 **Enter the first of the records shown in Figure 3.2.** Experiment with making corrections.

Press	F2	Moves to Edit screen.
Type	1011	
Type	Rappozi, Athony P.	(an intentional mistake)
Press	↵ ENTER	
Type	011092	
Type	Shipping	
Press	↵ ENTER	
Type	8.50	

You now correct the mistake you made when you entered the name.

Figure 3.2

Data for Employee Database File

EMPLOYEE NUMBER	EMPLOYEE NAME	DATE HIRED	DEPARTMENT NAME	PAY RATE	UNION MEMBER
1011	Rapoza, Anthony P.	01/10/92	Shipping	8.50	T
1013	McCormack, Nigel L.	01/15/92	Shipping	8.25	T
1016	Ackerman, David R.	02/04/92	Accounting	9.75	F
1017	Doi, Chang J.	02/05/92	Production	6.00	T
1020	Castle, Mark C.	03/04/92	Shipping	7.50	T
1022	Dunning, Lisa A.	03/12/92	Marketing	9.10	F
1025	Chaney, Joseph R.	03/23/92	Accounting	8.00	F
1026	Bender, Helen O.	04/12/92	Production	6.75	T
1029	Anderson, Mariane L.	04/18/92	Shipping	9.00	T
1030	Edwards, Kenneth J.	04/23/92	Production	8.60	T
1037	Baxter, Charles W.	05/05/92	Accounting	11.00	F
1041	Evans, John T.	05/19/92	Marketing	6.00	F
1056	Andrews, Robert M.	06/03/92	Marketing	9.00	F
1057	Dugan, Mary L.	06/10/92	Production	8.75	T
1066	Castleworth, Mary T.	07/05/92	Production	8.75	T

Press	↑ repeatedly	until you have moved back to NAME.
Type	Rapoza, Anthony P.	

Instead of typing the entire correct name, you could use the keys shown in Figure 3.2 to make the corrections. Feel free to experiment with these keys at this point.

Press	↵ ENTER repeatedly	until you have moved back to UNION.
Type	T	

3 **Make the entries for Record 2 (including some mistakes).** We will later use these mistakes to illustrate the process of correcting errors in existing records.

Type	1013	
Type	McCrmaack, Nigel L.	(an intentional mistake)
Press	↵ ENTER	
Type	011592	
Type	Shiping	(an intentional mistake)
Press	↵ ENTER	
Type	8.75	
Type	F	

4 **Add an extra record.** Use your own name as the employee name. Make up whatever data you want for the rest of the fields. Leave dBASE when you are done. Add the data as you did in the previous task and move on to the next record.

Select	"Exit"	from Exit menu.

5 **Restart dBASE and add the remaining records shown in Figure 3.2.**

Start	dBASE	as you did before.
Activate	EMPLOYEE	as you did before.
Press	F2	Moves to Edit screen.

TIP When you are adding records, if you inadvertently press ENTER while the highlight is in the first position of the first field of the form, dBASE assumes you have finished entering your data and returns you to the Control Center. If this happens, add the remaining records in the same fashion as you have been.

When you pressed F2 earlier to move to the Edit screen, the form on the screen was blank and you could begin adding your records. Because no records were in the file, dBASE assumed you wanted to add new records. This time, however, you already have some records in your file, so dBASE assumes you want change some of these records. We want to add records, however.

Select	"Add new records"	from Records menu.

Now add the rest of the records shown in Figure 3.2 as you did before. If you make any mistakes in entering a particular record and discover them while you are still working on the record, you can correct them using the same techniques you used to correct Anthony Rapoza's name. If you don't discover them in time, don't worry. The next task shows how to change existing records. ◄

TIP If you leave dBASE, you must reactivate the EMPLOYEE file, press F2, and then select "Add additional records" to resume adding your data.

Select	"Exit"	from Exit menu.

You do not need to add all the records in one sitting. ◄

6 **Correct the second record.**

Activate	EMPLOYEE	
Press	F2 once or twice	Moves to Edit screen.

Record 1 is currently on the screen, and you want to correct record 2.

Press	PAGE DOWN	Moves to record 2.
Type	McCormack, Nigel L.	as the new name.
Type	Shipping	as the new department.

> **TIP** While in Edit mode, if you make corrections to the last field in the last record in the file, you are asked if you wish to add additional records. Assuming that you do not, simply type the letter N (for No). You can then select the "Exit" option of the Exit menu.

Type	8.25	as the new pay rate.
Type	T	as the new value for UNION.
Select	"Exit"	from Exit menu.

Making corrections to the last field of the last record is a different situation. ◀

7 Mark the third record (the extra one you added) for deletion.

Activate	EMPLOYEE	
Press	F2 once or twice	Moves to Edit screen.

Record 1 is currently on the screen, and you want to delete record 3.

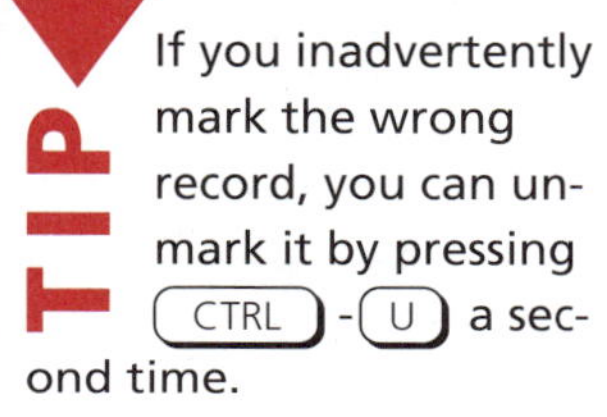

> **TIP** If you inadvertently mark the wrong record, you can unmark it by pressing CTRL-U a second time.

Press	PAGE DOWN twice	Moves to record 3.
Press	CTRL-U	Marks record for deletion. ◀
Select	"Exit"	from Exit menu.

8 Remove any marked records.

Activate	EMPLOYEE	
Press	F2 once or twice	Moves to Edit screen.
Select	"Erase marked records"	from Organize menu.

Remember that you can use the Organize menu on the Edit screen, the Browse screen, or the Database Design screen. Here you are using the one on the Edit screen, but it really doesn't matter which one you use. The marked records are now permanently removed.

Select	"Exit"	from Exit menu.

9 Display all the records in the EMPLOYEE database file.

Activate	EMPLOYEE	
Press	SHIFT-F9	(Hold the Shift key down while you press F9.)

If you look at the Control Center on your screen, you'll see "Quick Report: Shift-F9" on the screen. You don't have to be at the Control Center to use it, however. You can use it from the Edit or Browse screens just as well. If a printer is attached to your computer, you can print a copy of the report.

Select	"Begin printing"

If you don't have a printer or just don't want to print the report at this time, but you want to see what the report looks like, you can view it.

Select	"View report on screen"

If you view the report on the screen, you will see one screenful at a time. After each screenful is displayed, a message appears indicating that you can press Escape if you don't want to see any more or press the spacebar to see the next screenful. If you decide you don't want to print the report and you don't want to view it, press Escape and you are returned to the Control Center.

PROCEDURE SUMMARY

ACTIVATING A CATALOG

Select the "Use a different catalog" option of the Catalog menu and then select the desired catalog.	(your choice)

ACTIVATING A DATABASE FILE

Check to see if the desired database file appears above the line in the Data column. If not, select the database file and then select "Use file."	(your choice)

ADDING RECORDS TO A DATABASE FILE

Make sure the database file is active.	
Move to the Edit screen.	F2
If records are already in the file, select the "Add new records" option of the Records menu.	
Enter your data.	(your input)
Select the "Exit" option of the Exit menu.	

CHANGING RECORDS IN A DATABASE FILE

Make sure the database file is active.	
Move to the Edit screen.	F2

Bring the record you want to correct to the screen.	PAGE UP or PAGE DOWN
Make the necessary changes.	(your input)
If other records are to be changed, change them in the same way.	
Select the "Exit" option of the Exit menu.	

DELETING RECORDS FROM A DATABASE FILE

To mark records for deletion:

Make sure the database file is active.	
Move to the Edit screen.	F2
Bring the record you want to mark for deletion to the screen.	PAGE UP or PAGE DOWN
Mark the record for deletion.	CTRL-U
If other records are to be marked, mark them in the same way.	
If you have marked any record that should not be marked, bring the record to the screen and unmark it.	CTRL-U
Select the "Exit" option of the Exit menu.	

To permanently remove marked records:

Make sure the database file is active.	
Move to the Edit screen.	F2
Select the "Erase marked records" option of the Organize menu.	

LISTING RECORDS IN A DATABASE FILE

Make sure the database file is active.	
Select "Quick-Report."	SHIFT-F9
If you want to print a copy of the report, select "Begin printing."	
If you want to view the report on the screen, select "View report on screen."	

EXERCISES

1. Add the following data to the CHECK database file. When you enter the third check (check 111), enter the name of the payee as Etteson Company and enter the check amount as 25.55. After you have entered this check, enter a check that does not belong in the database. You may make up any data you want for this check. (We will use this later to illustrate the process of deleting records.) Then enter the remaining checks. Remember that you do not need to enter all the checks at once.

CHECKNUM	DATE	PAYEE	AMOUNT	EXPENSE	TAXDED
109	01/19/92	Oak Apartments	750.00	Household	T
102	01/05/92	Sav-Mor Groceries	85.00	Food	F
111	01/19/92	Edison Company	55.25	Household	F
106	01/12/92	Performing Arts	25.00	Charity	T
105	01/12/92	Union Oil	22.75	Automobile	T
101	01/05/92	American Express	45.30	Entertainment	T
107	01/19/92	Sav-Mor Groceries	64.95	Food	F
108	01/19/92	Amber Inn	22.45	Entertainment	T
104	01/12/92	Brady's Shoes	69.50	Personal	F
110	01/19/92	Standard Oil	33.16	Automobile	T
103	01/05/92	Pacific Telephone	23.72	Household	F

2. Correct the data for check 111 by changing the name of the payee to Edison Company and the check amount to 55.25.
3. Delete the extra check that does not belong in the database file (the one you added in the exercises for the last topic). Permanently remove this check from the file.
4. Display the data in the CHECK database file.

Backing Up Your Database

CONCEPTS

A database file can be damaged. A power failure or a general computer failure, for example, that occurs while you are updating a database can destroy the database. As a safeguard, you should periodically make a copy of your database file. This copy is called a **backup copy**, and the database file itself is called the **live copy.**

Making a Backup Copy 32

You can make backup copies while you are in dBASE, but a simpler method is to use the DOS COPY command after you have exited dBASE. You use the COPY command to copy the live version of the database file over a backup version. A separate related file, called the production index file, should also be backed up. The production index file has the same name as the database file, but a different extension. The extension for a database file is .DBF, whereas the extension for the corresponding production index file is .MDX. (Thus the production index file for EMPLOYEE.DBF is EMPLOYEE.MDX.)

Restoring a Database File from a Backup Copy 

If you discover a problem with a database file, you can use the same DOS COPY command to copy the backup versions over the live ones. This effectively returns the database file to the state it was in when you made the last backup.

TUTORIAL

In this tutorial, you make a backup copy of the EMPLOYEE database file and the corresponding production index file. You then use these backup copies to recover the data in the file.

1 Make a backup copy of the EMPLOYEE database file and production index file. Call the backup copies EMPBACK.DBF and EMPBACK.MDX, respectively. Assume that the database file is on the diskette in drive A and the backup copy is to be placed on this same diskette.

Select	"Quit to DOS"	from Exit menu of Control Center.
Type	COPY A:EMPLOYEE.DBF A:EMPBACK.DBF	

Press	↵ ENTER

You should see the message "1 file(s) copied."

Type	COPY A:EMPLOYEE.MDX A:EMPBACK.MDX
Press	↵ ENTER

TIP You may wish to place the backup copy on a separate disk or diskette. If you do, replace the A that precedes the name of the backup file with the appropriate drive designation.

You should see the message "1 file(s) copied." This approach uses the DOS COPY command to make the copy. The choice of the names EMPBACK.DBF and EMPBACK.MDX was purely arbitrary. You can choose whatever names you wish, but make sure you can easily recognize them. ◀

2 **Recover the EMPLOYEE database file.** You discovered a problem in the EMPLOYEE database file. Recover the file by copying the backup version over the live version.

Select	"Quit to DOS"	from Exit menu of Control Center.
Type	COPY A:EMPBACK.DBF A:EMPLOYEE.DBF	
Press	↵ ENTER	
Type	COPY A:EMPBACK.MDX A:EMPLOYEE.MDX	
Press	↵ ENTER	

PROCEDURE SUMMARY

MAKING A BACKUP COPY

Select "Quit to DOS" from the Exit menu of the Control Center.	
Type COPY and press the spacebar.	COPY SPACEBAR
Enter the name of the live database file.	(your input) SPACEBAR
Enter the name of the backup database file.	(your input) ↵ ENTER
Enter the name of the live production index file.	(your input) SPACEBAR
Enter the name of the backup production index file.	(your input) ↵ ENTER

RESTORING A DATABASE FILE FROM A BACKUP COPY

Select "Quit to DOS" from the Exit menu of the Control Center.	
Type COPY and press the spacebar.	COPY [SPACEBAR]
Enter the name of the backup database file.	(your input) [SPACEBAR]
Enter the name of the live database file.	(your input) [↵ENTER]
Enter the name of the backup production index file.	(your input) [SPACEBAR]
Enter the name of the live production index file.	(your input) [↵ENTER]

EXERCISES

1. Make a backup copy of the CHECK database file and corresponding production index file. Call them CHECKBCK.DBF and CHECKBCK.MDX, respectively.
2. Use these backup copies to recover the data in the CHECK database file.

Querying a Database

CONCEPTS One of the major benefits of a database management system like dBASE is the ease with which you can retrieve specific data in a database. This is often called *querying* a database. (Generally, to query means to ask for information; specifically, you are asking dBASE for information.) You access data in a file by using what dBASE terms **queries**. When creating queries, you specify the conditions that the data you want must satisfy. For example, you might specify that the pay rate of certain employees must be $6.00. You can also specify the fields that you want included. You might choose, for example, to only include the name, department, and pay rate.

Creating a Query 40

To create a query, you use the Query Design screen (Figure 5.1). Near the top of this screen is a **File skeleton**. It lists the name of the database file together with all the fields in the file. You use this skeleton to define the conditions for your queries, that is, the requirements that must be satisfied in order for a record to be displayed. Near the bottom of the screen is the **View skeleton**. It specifies the fields that will be included, that is, the fields that will be displayed when you see the results of the query.

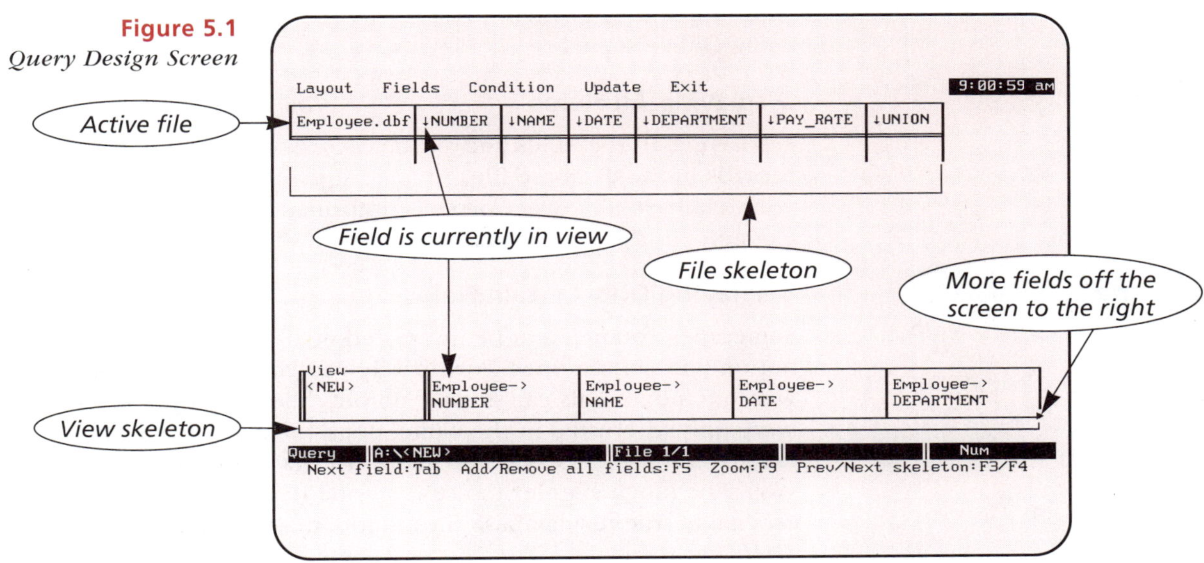

Figure 5.1
Query Design Screen

In the File skeleton, notice the down arrows in front of the fields. A down arrow in front of a field indicates that it is included in the View skeleton. Initially all fields are included in the View skeleton, so all fields in the File skeleton will have these down arrows. This need not always be the case, however.

On the screen in Figure 5.1, the View skeleton has a right-pointing arrow at the far right-hand end. This indicates that additional fields are off the right-hand edge of the screen. Similarly a left-pointing arrow at the left-hand edge of the screen indicates additional fields in that direction.

There are two important types of movements within the Query Design screen. The first type is movement within a skeleton. Pressing the TAB key takes you one field to the right. Pressing SHIFT-TAB (holding the SHIFT key down while you press the TAB key) moves you one field to the left. In either case, if you move to a field that is not currently displayed on the screen, the fields are shifted so that the field to which you are moving is visible.

The second type is movement from one skeleton to another. Pressing F4 moves you to the next skeleton on the screen. Pressing F3 moves you back to the prior skeleton.

Applying a Query 40

When you have finished designing a query, you would like to see the results. This is called *applying* a query. All you need to do is press F2. This takes you to the Browse screen where the results of your query are displayed. (Remember that F2 takes you to either the Browse or the Edit screen. If it takes you to the Edit screen, all you need to do is press F2 a second time to view the Browse screen.) At the Browse screen, only the records that satisfy your conditions are displayed and only the fields that you selected are included.

Printing the Results 40

Having applied the query, you can see the results on the screen. If you want the results printed, press SHIFT-F9. The results are then printed using Quick Report.

Displaying All Fields 40

Displaying all the fields and all the records produces a list of all the records in the database file. Such a list gives you complete details about your database file. Every piece of information about every employee, for example, in the EMPLOYEE database file would appear on such a list.

Displaying Only Certain Fields 40

Sometimes you may not be interested in all the fields in your database file, but only in certain ones. Fortunately you can specify those fields that you want included. This can greatly simplify the list. Suppose, for example, you were only interested in the name, department, and pay rate for the employees in the EMPLOYEE file. A list that only included these fields would be much simpler to use than one that included all fields. This is especially true for database files that contain large numbers of fields.

The View skeleton (the list of fields near the bottom of the Query Design screen) indicates which fields are part of the view, that is, which fields you see when you apply the query. Initially the View skeleton contains all fields. There are several ways to change the skeleton so that it contains precisely the fields you want. The simplest way relies on the following characteristics of the F5 key:

1. If the highlight is under a field name in the File skeleton and that field is currently in the View skeleton, pressing F5 removes the field. If the field is not in the View skeleton, pressing F5 adds the highlighted field to the end of the list of fields currently in the View skeleton.
2. If the highlight is under the name of the database file in the File skeleton and if there are fields currently in the View skeleton, pressing F5 removes all fields. (You might need to press F5 twice to remove all fields.) If no fields are currently in the View skeleton, pressing F5 adds all fields.

> **TIP** If you make a mistake, just start over. Move the highlight back under the database filename, use F5 to delete all fields, and then reselect the fields.

You can always use these properties of the F5 key to construct the precise View skeleton you want. First, you move the highlight under the database filename in the File skeleton and then use F5 to remove all fields. Next you add the fields in the order you want. To add any field, move the highlight under it in the File skeleton and press F5. ◄

Returning to the Control Center 41

You have two choices when you return from the Database Design screen to the Control Center. You can save your work or abandon it. That is, you can choose whether or not you want to save the query that you have created. Later, you will see special situations where you will want to save a query. For now, however, do not save any queries.

TUTORIAL

In this tutorial, you first learn how to move around on the Query Design screen. Then you display all the fields and all the records in the EMPLOYEE database file. Next you restrict the fields to be displayed.

1 Activate the EMPLOYEE database file and move to the Query Design screen.

Activate	EMPLOYEE	
Select	<create>	in Queries column.

You should now see the Query Design screen (Figure 5.1).

2 Move to the View skeleton and then back to the File skeleton.

Press	F4	Moves to View skeleton.
Press	F3	Moves to File skeleton.

> **TIP** If you are on the last column, pressing TAB takes you back to the first column. If you are on the first column, pressing SHIFT-TAB takes you to the last column.

3 Move to the NAME column in the File skeleton and then back to the column labeled EMPLOYEE.dbf.

Press	TAB twice	Moves to NAME column.
Press	SHIFT-TAB twice	Moves back to EMPLOYEE.dbf column. ◀

4 Display all the records in the EMPLOYEE database file and print your results.

To display all records, do not enter any conditions to restrict the records to be displayed.

Press	F2	Applies query.
Press	SHIFT-F9	Produces Quick Report.
Select	"Begin printing"	
Select	"Transfer to Query Design"	from Exit menu.

You are now returned directly to the Query Design screen.

5 Display the name, department, and pay rate for all employees.

Press	TAB or SHIFT-TAB as necessary	Moves highlight under Employee.dbf.
Press	F5	Removes all fields from View skeleton.
Press	TAB twice	Moves highlight to NAME column.
Press	F5	Adds NAME to View skeleton.
Press	TAB twice	Moves highlight to DEPARTMENT column.
Press	F5	Adds DEPARTMENT to View skeleton.
Press	TAB	Moves highlight to PAY_RATE column.
Press	F5	Adds PAY_RATE to View skeleton.
Press	F2	Applies query.

The results include only the desired fields (Figure 5.2). ◀

> **TIP** The last column on the Browse screen often looks a little odd because dBASE always sizes the last column so that it occupies whatever space is left on the screen. Fortunately, if you print these results (using Shift-F9), you will not see this strange spacing.

Figure 5.2
Browse Screen

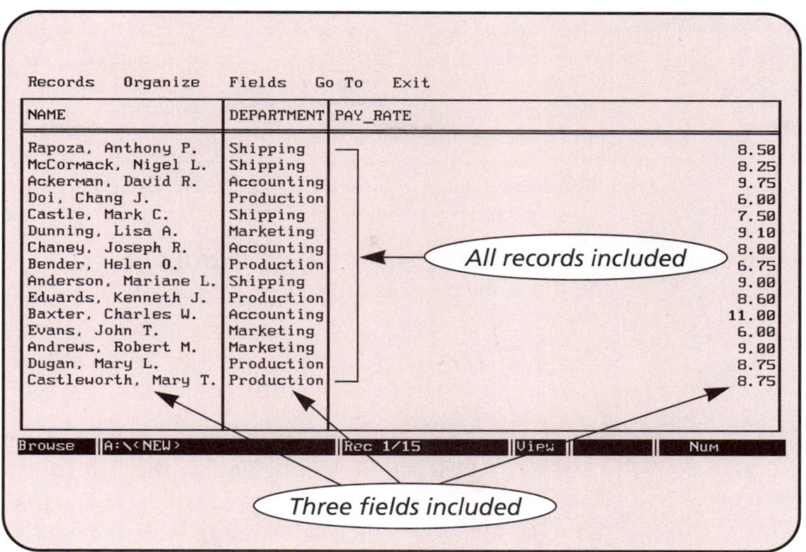

Press	SHIFT - F9	Produces Quick Report.
Select	"Begin printing"	
Select	"Transfer to Query Design"	from Exit menu.

TIP Sometimes you need to press F5 twice to clear out the View skeleton, and other times you only need to press it once. Don't worry about this. All you really need to do is keep pressing F5 until the View skeleton disappears.

6 **Display the department, name, and pay rate for all employees.** This is the same as the previous task, except that the fields are in a different order.

Press	TAB or SHIFT - TAB as necessary	Moves the highlight under Employee.dbf.
Press	F5 twice ◀	Removes all fields from View skeleton.
Press	TAB four times	Moves highlight to DEPARTMENT column.
Press	F5	Adds DEPARTMENT to View skeleton.
Press	SHIFT - TAB twice	Moves highlight to NAME column.
Press	F5	Adds NAME to View skeleton.
Press	TAB three times	Moves highlight to PAY_RATE column.
Press	F5	Adds PAY_RATE to View skeleton.

Press	F2	Applies query.
Press	SHIFT - F9	Produces Quick Report.
Select	"Begin printing"	
Select	"Transfer to Query Design"	from Exit menu.

7 Return to the Control Center.

Select	"Abandon changes and exit"	from Exit menu.
Select	"Yes"	Abandons query.

You are now returned to the Control Center.

PROCEDURE SUMMARY

CREATING A QUERY

Activate the appropriate database file.	
Select <create> in the Queries column.	

APPLYING A QUERY

Apply the query.	F2
Select "Transfer to Query Design" from the Exit menu to return to the Query Design screen.	

PRINTING THE RESULTS

Select "Quick Report."	SHIFT - F9
Select "Begin printing."	

DISPLAYING ALL FIELDS

Do not change View skeleton.	

DISPLAYING ONLY CERTAIN FIELDS

Remove all fields from the View skeleton.	
Add the desired fields to the View skeleton in the appropriate order.	

To remove all fields from the View skeleton:

Move the highlight under the name of the database file.	TAB or SHIFT - TAB
Erase the View skeleton.	F5

To add a field to the View skeleton:

Move the highlight under the field.	TAB or SHIFT - TAB
Add the field to the View skeleton.	F5

RETURNING TO THE CONTROL CENTER

Select "Abandon changes and exit" from the Exit menu.

Select "Yes" to abandon query.

EXERCISES

1. Display all the records and all the fields in the CHECK database file.
2. Display the Check Number, Date, Payee, and the Check Amount fields for all checks.
3. Display the Date field, and then the Check Number, Payee, and Check Amount fields for all checks.

Using Conditions

> **TIP** When you enter a value containing letters, be very careful about using upper- or lowercase. For example, if you are searching for records whose DEPARTMENT is Accounting and you enter ACCOUNTING, dBASE will not find any records because it considers ACCOUNTING to be different from Accounting.

CONCEPTS

In many cases, when you query a database, you are only interested in those records that satisfy some condition. (A **condition** is an expression that is either true or false.) Suppose, for example, that you only wanted information about those employees whose pay rate is greater than $6.00. What you really want is to display only those employees for whom the condition "pay rate is greater than 6.00" is true. It would be very cumbersome to have to scan through a report containing all the records just to find those that satisfy your condition. Thus the ability to display only those records that satisfy a condition is crucial in the query process.

Using a Condition (52)

To enter a condition on the Query Design screen, type the desired value in the appropriate column.

Using CHARACTER Fields in Conditions (53)

To use a value for a CHARACTER field in a condition, it must be enclosed in quotation marks. Three special conditions are available for CHARACTER fields: exact match, pattern matching, and sounds like.

Exact match. To find an exact match, simply type the desired character string (collection of characters) in the desired column. The character string must be enclosed in quotation marks. ◄

Pattern matching. To find entries that match a given pattern, use the word LIKE, followed by the desired pattern. In specifying the pattern, you can use two special symbols, called *wildcards*. (These, incidentally, are the same wildcards you can use in DOS.) The first of these is the asterisk (*), which represents any collection of characters. The other is the question mark (?), which represents a single character. The pattern must be enclosed in quotes.

To find all employees named Mary, for example, you must find all employees whose name contains Mary somewhere within it. Using LIKE "*Mary*" in your condition indicates that you are looking for names that have any collection of characters, followed by Mary, followed by any other collection of characters.

Because the question mark represents only a single character, using LIKE "?Mary?" would be true only for those names that consist of a single character, followed by Mary, followed by another single character. Although this pattern would not be appropriate for the example here because the names you want have more than a single character before and after Mary, the question mark can come in handy in a few situations. The vast majority of the time, however, you use the asterisk.

Sounds like. You can even find records if you just know what a character string is supposed to sound like. Let's suppose you do not know how to spell an employee's name, but you know how the name sounds. To find such employees, the condition would be SOUNDS LIKE, followed by your character string.

Using NUMERIC Fields in Conditions 53

The only difference between using a numeric field and using a character field in a condition is that you do not enclose numeric values in quotes.

Using Operators 53

TIP: If you do not enter an operator, dBASE assumes that you mean "equals."

When you type a value, you are really using = (equals). For example, if you type 6.00 in the PAY_RATE column, you are asking for all employees for whom the pay rate *equals* 6.00. "Equals" is called an operator. You can use several other operators besides "equals" (see Table 6.1). (Note that the last two operators listed in the figure are the special-purpose operators for CHARACTER fields that we discussed earlier.) ◀

Table 6.1
Operators Available for Conditions

OPERATOR	MEANING
=	Equals
>	Greater than
>=	Greater than or equal to
<	Less than
<=	Less than or equal to
<>	Not equal to (can also use #)
LIKE	Matches the given pattern
SOUNDS LIKE	Sounds like the given entry

TIP: When you type values for conditions involving CHARACTER fields, be careful to use the same combination of upper- and lowercase as was used in the data that was entered into the database. If you type "MARKETING" (all uppercase) instead of "Marketing," for example, the effect of the comparison operators would not be as shown in Table 6.3, but rather as shown in Table 6.4. This is certainly not what you would want.

With the exception of LOGICAL fields (which are discussed separately), conditions consist of a field, a comparison operator, and a value. Table 6.2 lists the comparison operators and indicates which records would be selected, assuming the selected field is PAY_RATE, a NUMERIC field. If the selected field is DEPARTMENT, a CHARACTER field, the effect of the various operators would be as shown in Table 6.3. (In this case, since the only departments in the database are Accounting, Marketing, Production, and Shipping, the table indicates the specific departments that would be selected.) Note that "greater than" for CHARACTER fields effectively means "comes later alphabetically." ◀

Table 6.2

Effect of Comparison Operators When Field Is PAY_RATE

Symbol	Meaning	Value	True for records on which
=	Equal To	6.75	pay rate is exactly 6.75
<=	Less Than or Equal To	6.75	pay rate is 6.75 or below
<	Less Than	6.75	pay rate is below 6.75
>	Greater Than	6.75	pay rate is above 6.75
>=	Greater Than or Equal To	6.75	pay rate is 6.75 or above
<>	Not Equal To	6.75	pay rate is anything but 6.75

Table 6.3

Effect of Comparison Operators When Field Is DEPARTMENT

Symbol	Meaning	Value	True for records on which
=	Equal To	"Marketing"	department is Marketing
<=	Less Than or Equal To	"Marketing"	department is Accounting or Marketing
<	Less Than	"Marketing"	department is Accounting
>	Greater Than	"Marketing"	department is Production or Shipping
>=	Greater Than or Equal To	"Marketing"	department is Marketing, Production, or Shipping
<>	Not Equal To	"Marketing"	department is Accounting, Production, or Shipping

Using LOGICAL Fields in Conditions

53

You use LOGICAL fields (fields whose type is "Logical") in conditions in just about the same way as any other type of field. The only difference is that the values you place in the column can be only the letter T (for true) or the letter F (for false). Note that you must enclose these letters between periods (that is, .T. and .F.).

Using DATE Fields in Conditions

You can use dates in conditions by enclosing the dates in curly brackets ({ }). These are usually called braces.

Table 6.4
Effect of Comparison Operators When Field Is DEPARTMENT

Symbol	Meaning	Value	True for records on which
=	Equal To	"MARKETING"	none
<=	Less Than or Equal To	"MARKETING"	department is Accounting
<	Less Than	"MARKETING"	department is Accounting
>	Greater Than	"MARKETING"	department is Marketing, Production, or Shipping
>=	Greater Than or Equal To	"MARKETING"	department is Marketing, Production, or Shipping
<>	Not Equal To	"MARKETING"	department is Accounting, Marketing, Production, or Shipping

Combining Conditions with AND

54

The conditions discussed so far are called **simple conditions.** They consist of a single field, a comparison operator, and a value. (In the special case of LOGICAL fields, they consist solely of a single field.) In some cases, simple conditions are not sufficient for your needs. Suppose, for example, you want to list all the employees in the Accounting department whose pay rate is $11.00. This involves more than just a simple condition.

Fortunately simple conditions can be combined using AND to form **compound conditions.** This is exactly what you need. You want all employees for whom the compound condition "DEPARTMENT equals Accounting *and* pay rate equals 11.00" is true. To combine conditions with AND, type both conditions on the same line.

Combining Conditions with OR

The same discussion applies to forming compound conditions by combining simple conditions with OR. The condition "DEPARTMENT equals Accounting *or* pay rate is less than 9.00" is true for those employees who are in the Accounting department or whose pay rate is less than $9.00 (or both). To combine conditions with OR, type the conditions on separate lines.

TUTORIAL

In this tutorial, you use conditions to restrict the records that are displayed.

Display all fields for the employee whose number is 1030.

Activate	EMPLOYEE	
Select	<create>	in Queries column.

Press	TAB	Moves to NUMBER column.
Type	"1030"	

Remember to enclose values for CHARACTER fields in quotes.

Press	↵ ENTER	Completes condition.
Press	F2	Applies query.

Now you can print the results.

Press	SHIFT - F9	Produces Quick Report.
Select	"Begin printing"	
Select	"Transfer to Query Design"	from Exit menu.

If you go back to the Control Center after you have seen the results of your query and later begin a new query, you start fresh—no conditions are in place. If, however, you go directly to the Query Design screen from the Browse screen, the conditions you entered previously are still there. You must make sure that you clear out the previous entries before entering the conditions for your next query. If you do not, you will not get the results you are expecting. To clear out an entry, move the highlight to it and press Control-Y (hold down the Control key and type the letter Y). If you have returned to the Query Design screen directly from the Browse screen, "1030" is still in the NUMBER column.

Press	CTRL - Y	Clears out previous entry.

2 Display all fields for all employees whose pay rate is 6.00.

Press	TAB four times	Moves to PAY_RATE column.

If you started this query from scratch, you would need to press Tab five times to move to the PAY_RATE column.

Type	6.00	
Press	↵ ENTER	Completes condition.
Press	F2	Applies query.

Now you can print the results.

Press	SHIFT - F9	Produces Quick Report.
Select	"Begin printing"	

Select	"Transfer to Query Design"	from Exit menu.
Press	CTRL-Y	Clears out previous entry.

3 Display all fields for all employees whose pay rate is greater than 9.00. Make sure the highlight is in the PAY_RATE column. If you started this query from scratch, press Tab five times to get it there.

Type	>9.00	
Press	↵ ENTER	Completes condition.
Press	F2	Applies query.

Now you can print the results.

Press	SHIFT-F9	Produces Quick Report.
Select	"Begin printing"	
Select	"Transfer to Query Design"	from Exit menu.
Press	CTRL-Y	Clears out previous entry.

4 Display the name, department, and pay rate for those employees whose department is Shipping.

Press	SHIFT-TAB	Moves highlight to DEPARTMENT.

If you started this query from scratch, press Tab four times instead of pressing Shift-Tab.

Type	"Shipping"	
Press	↵ ENTER	Completes condition.

(When you type the word "Shipping," you must type an uppercase "S" and the rest of the word in lowercase.)

Press	SHIFT-TAB four times	Moves highlight under Employee.dbf.
Press	F5	Removes all fields from View skeleton.
Press	TAB twice	Moves highlight to NAME column.
Press	F5	Adds NAME to View skeleton.

Press	TAB twice	Moves highlight to DEPARTMENT column.
Press	F5	Adds DEPARTMENT to View skeleton.
Press	TAB	Moves highlight to PAY_RATE column.
Press	F5	Adds PAY_RATE to View skeleton.
Press	F2	Applies query.

Now you can print the results.

Press	SHIFT-F9	Produces Quick Report.
Select	"Begin printing"	
Select	"Transfer to Query Design"	from Exit menu.
Press	SHIFT-TAB	Moves to DEPARTMENT column.
Press	CTRL-Y	Clears out previous entry.

Before you go on, you should restore the View skeleton to its original state.

Press	SHIFT-TAB	Moves cursor under Employee.dbf.
Press	F5 twice	Erases View skeleton.
Press	F5	Restores complete View skeleton.

5 Display all the fields for employees named Mary.

Press	TAB twice	Moves highlight to NAME.
Type	LIKE "*Mary*"	
Press	↵ ENTER	Completes condition.
Press	F2	Applies query.

Now you can print the results.

Press	SHIFT-F9	Produces Quick Report.
Select	"Begin printing"	

Select	"Transfer to Query Design"	from Exit menu.
Press	CTRL-Y	Clears out previous entry.

6 **Display all the fields for employees whose name sounds like "Doy."** If you started this query from scratch, press Tab twice to move the highlight to NAME. If you are continuing from the previous query, the highlight should already be there.

Type	SOUNDS LIKE "DOY"	
Press	↵ ENTER	Completes condition.

Because you are only interested in the sound of the name, it doesn't matter whether you use upper- or lowercase.

Press	F2	Applies query.

Now you can print the results.

Press	SHIFT-F9	Produces Quick Report.
Select	"Begin printing"	
Select	"Transfer to Query Design"	from Exit menu.
Press	CTRL-Y	Clears out previous entry.

7 **Display all the fields for employees who are in the union (UNION is true).**

Press	TAB four times	Moves to UNION column.

If you started this query from scratch, press Tab five times to move the highlight to UNION.

Type	.T.	
Press	↵ ENTER	Completes condition.
Press	F2	Applies query.

Now you can print the results.

Press	SHIFT-F9	Produces Quick Report.
Select	"Begin printing"	
Select	"Transfer to Query Design"	from Exit menu.
Press	CTRL-Y	Clears out previous entry.

8 Display all the fields for employees who were hired after March 1, 1992. If you started this query from scratch, press Tab three times to move the highlight to DATE.

Type	>{3/01/92}	
Press	↵ ENTER	Completes condition.
Press	F2	Applies query.

Now you can print the results.

Press	SHIFT - F9	Produces Quick Report.
Select	"Begin printing"	
Select	"Transfer to Query Design"	from Exit menu.
Press	CTRL - Y	Clears out previous entry.

9 Display the employees who are in the Accounting department and whose pay rate is more than 9.00. Because this condition involves AND, you must place both conditions on the same line. If you started this query from scratch, press Tab four times to move the highlight to DEPARTMENT.

Type	"Accounting"	
Press	↵ ENTER	Completes condition.
Press	TAB	Moves to PAY_RATE column.
Type	>9.00	
Press	↵ ENTER	Completes condition.
Press	F2	Applies query.

Now you can print the results.

Press	SHIFT - F9	Produces Quick Report.
Select	"Begin printing"	
Select	"Transfer to Query Design"	from Exit menu.
Press	CTRL - Y	Clears out previous entry.
Press	SHIFT - TAB	Moves to DEPARTMENT column.
Press	CTRL - Y	Clears out previous entry.

In most cases, the conditions involve different columns. If they involve the same column, type both conditions in the column, but separate them with a comma.

10 Display the employees who are in the Accounting department or who belong to the union (or both). Because this condition involves OR, you must place the conditions on separate lines. If you started this query from scratch, press Tab four times to move the highlight to DEPARTMENT.

Type	"Accounting"	
Press	↵ ENTER	Completes condition.
Press	TAB twice	Moves to UNION column.
Press	↓	Creates extra line.
Type	.T.	
Press	↵ ENTER	Completes condition.
Press	F2	Applies query.

Now you can print the results.

Press	SHIFT - F9	Produces Quick Report.
Select	"Begin printing"	
Select	"Transfer to Query Design"	from Exit menu.
Press	CTRL - Y	Clears out previous entry.
Press	↑	Removes extra line.

To remove the extra line, you *must* clear out the previous entry before pressing the Up Arrow.

Press	SHIFT - TAB twice	Moves to DEPARTMENT column.
Press	CTRL - Y	Clears out previous entry.

PROCEDURE SUMMARY

USING A CONDITION

Move to the column for the condition.	TAB or SHIFT - TAB
Enter the condition.	(your input)
Apply the query.	F2

USING CHARACTER FIELDS IN CONDITIONS

To find an exact match:

Enter the desired character string (enclosed in quotation marks).	(your input)

To find entries that match a given pattern:

Type LIKE and press the spacebar.	LIKE SPACEBAR
Enter the desired pattern. You can use two wildcards. An asterisk (*) represents any collection of characters. A question mark (?) represents a single character. The pattern must be enclosed in quotes.	(your input), *, ?

To find entries that sound like a particular character string:

Type SOUNDS LIKE and press the Spacebar.	SOUNDS LIKE SPACEBAR
Enter the character string enclosed in quotes.	(your input)

USING NUMERIC FIELDS IN CONDITIONS

Enter the desired number. Do not enclose it in quotation marks.	(your input)

USING OPERATORS

Type the operator (=, >, >=, <, <=, <>, LIKE, SOUNDS LIKE).	(your choice)
Press the spacebar.	SPACEBAR
Enter the value.	(your input)

USING LOGICAL FIELDS IN CONDITIONS

Enter true or false.	.T. or .F.

USING DATE FIELDS IN CONDITIONS

Type a left brace ({).	{
Type the date.	(your input)
Type a right brace (}).	}

COMBINING CONDITIONS WITH AND	Enter the conditions on the same line. If they are in the same column, separate them by commas.	(your input)
COMBINING CONDITIONS WITH OR	Enter the first condition.	(your input)
	Move down a line.	↓
	Enter the second condition.	(your input)

EXERCISES

1. Display the record for Check Number 108.
2. Display the record that contains the check written in the amount of $69.50.
3. Display the records for all checks written for Entertainment. Include the Check Number, Payee, Check Amount, and Expense Type fields.
4. Display the records for all checks written for Sav-Mor Groceries.
5. Display the records for all checks written to a payee whose name contains the word "Oil."
6. Display the records for all checks written to a payee whose name sounds like "Ember."
7. Display the records for all checks written that are tax deductible.
8. Display the records of all checks written for Entertainment with a check amount greater than $25.00.
9. Display the records for all checks written for Household Expenses or checks that were written for Food Expense.

TOPIC 7

Calculating Statistics

CONCEPTS

Five types of statistical calculations, also called **summary operators**, are available in dBASE: average, count, maximum, minimum, and sum. To use one of these operators, simply type it in the desired column. We will focus on average, count, and sum. The use of maximum and minimum is similar.

Counting Records 59

Sometimes you need to count all the records in a database file. At other times, you need to count only those records that satisfy some condition. For example, you might need to find out how many employees are currently in the Accounting department.

Calculating a Sum 60

Another statistic you need to be able to calculate is a sum (total). You often need to calculate the total of values in a certain field. Sometimes you need to calculate the total for all records; in other cases, you want only those records that satisfy a given condition. To find out the total payroll cost for one hour's work in the Accounting department, for example, you would like to find the sum of the pay rates for those records on which the department is Accounting.

Calculating an Average 60

Although in some cases it is important to calculate a sum, in others it is more important to calculate an average. Rather than the total of the pay rates of all employees in the Accounting department, for example, you might prefer to calculate the average pay rate.

Grouping 60

Suppose that you want to break the average pay rates down by department. That is, you would like to see the average pay rate for all employees in Accounting, the average pay rate for all employees in Marketing, and so on. This process is known as **grouping,** and you would say that you *group* employees by department.

TUTORIAL

In this tutorial, you calculate a variety of statistics concerning the EMPLOYEE database file.

> **TIP** It doesn't really matter whether you count employee numbers, names, or anything else. Thus you could put COUNT in any column. In general, you put it in whatever column is most convenient.

1 Count the number of employees in the Accounting department.

Activate	EMPLOYEE	
Select	<create>	in Queries column.
Press	TAB	Moves to NUMBER column.
Type	COUNT	
Press	↵ ENTER	Completes entry. ◀
Press	TAB three times	Moves to DEPARTMENT column.
Type	"Accounting"	
Press	↵ ENTER	Completes condition.
Press	F2	Applies query.

Your screen should then look like Figure 7.1. The count is displayed in the NUMBER column as you requested. All the other columns remain blank.

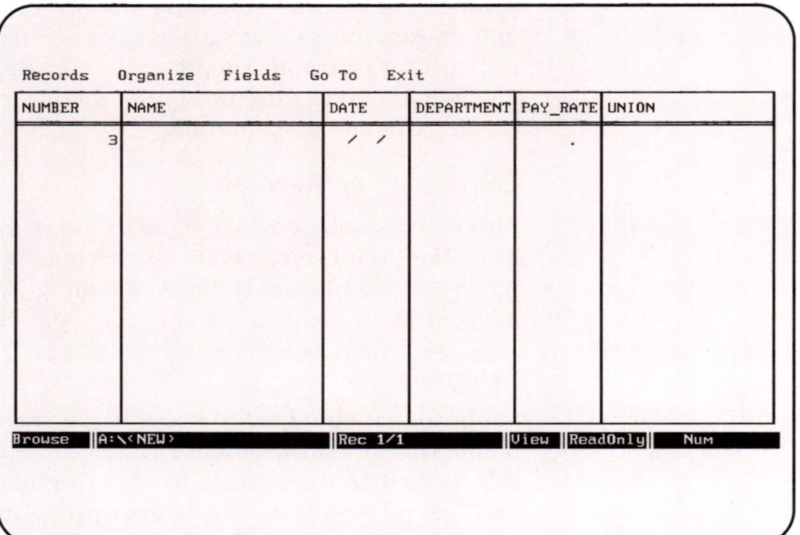

Figure 7.1
Query Design Screen

Select	"Transfer to Query Design"	from Exit menu.
Press	CTRL-Y	Clears out previous entry.
Press	SHIFT-TAB three times	Moves to NUMBER column.
Press	CTRL-Y	Clears out previous entry.

2 **Calculate the sum of all the pay rates.**

Press	TAB four times	Moves to PAY_RATE column.
Type	SUM	
Press	↵ ENTER	Completes entry.
Press	F2	Applies query.
Select	"Transfer to Query Design"	from Exit menu.
Press	CTRL-Y	Clears out previous entry.

3 **Calculate the sum of all the pay rates for the employees in the Accounting department.** If you are continuing from the previous query, your highlight should already be in the PAY_RATE column. If you are starting from scratch, press Tab five times to get it there.

Type	SUM	
Press	↵ ENTER	Completes condition.
Press	SHIFT-TAB	Moves to DEPARTMENT column.
Type	"Accounting"	
Press	↵ ENTER	Completes condition.
Press	F2	Applies query.
Select	"Transfer to Query Design"	from Exit menu.
Press	CTRL-Y	Clears out previous entry.
Press	TAB	Moves to PAY_RATE column.
Press	CTRL-Y	Clears out previous entry.

4 **Calculate the average pay rate for all employees.** If you are continuing from the previous query, your highlight should already be in the PAY_RATE column. If you are starting from scratch, press Tab five times to get it there.

Type	AVG	
Press	↵ ENTER	Completes entry.
Press	F2	Applies query.
Select	"Transfer to Query Design"	from Exit menu.
Press	CTRL - Y	Clears out previous entry.

5 Calculate the average pay rate for employees in the Accounting department. If you are continuing from the previous query, your highlight should already be in the PAY_RATE column. If you are starting from scratch, press Tab five times to get it there.

Type	AVG	
Press	↵ ENTER	Completes condition.
Press	SHIFT - TAB	Moves to DEPARTMENT column.
Type	"Accounting"	
Press	↵ ENTER	Completes condition.
Press	F2	Applies query.
Select	"Transfer to Query Design"	from Exit menu.
Press	CTRL - Y	Clears out previous entry.
Press	TAB	Moves to PAY_RATE column.
Press	CTRL - Y	Clears out previous entry.

6 Calculate the average pay rate for each department. If you are continuing from the previous query, your highlight should already be in the PAY_RATE column. If you are starting from scratch, press Tab five times to get it there.

Type	AVG	
Press	↵ ENTER	Completes condition.
Press	SHIFT - TAB	Moves to DEPARTMENT column.
Type	GROUP BY	
Press	↵ ENTER	Completes entry.

This indicates that employees are to be grouped by department.

Press	F2	Applies query.

When you apply this query, you see one line for each department. There is a line on which the department is Accounting, one on which it is Marketing, and so on. Each of these lines also includes the average pay rate for all employees in that department (Figure 7.2).

Figure 7.2
Browse Screen

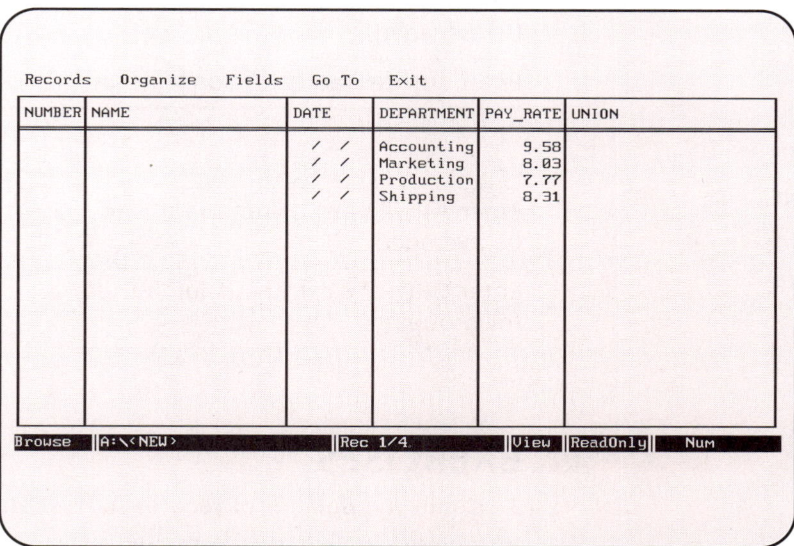

TIP To delete the other columns, return to the Query Design screen and modify the View skeleton so that it contains only DEPARTMENT and PAY_RATE.

Select	"Transfer to Query Design"	from Exit menu.
Press	CTRL-Y	Clears out previous entry.
Press	TAB	Moves to PAY_RATE column.
Press	CTRL-Y	Clears out previous entry.

You may decide that you would rather not have any columns displayed other than DEPARTMENT and PAY_RATE. ◄

PROCEDURE SUMMARY

COUNTING RECORDS

Enter COUNT in any column.	COUNT
Enter any desired condition.	(your input)

CALCULATING A SUM

Enter SUM in any column that is to be totaled.	SUM
Enter any desired condition.	(your input)

CALCULATING AN AVERAGE

Enter AVG in any column that is to be averaged.	AVG
Enter any desired condition.	(your input)

GROUPING

Enter AVG in any column that is to be averaged.	AVG
Enter GROUP BY in the column used for grouping.	GROUP BY

EXERCISES

1. Count the number of records in the CHECK database file.
2. Sum the check amount for all checks written.
3. Sum the amounts for the checks written for Household expenses.
4. Average the check amount for all checks written.
5. Average the check amount for all checks written for Entertainment.
6. Average the check amount for each expense category.

Checkpoint 1

What You Should Know

- ✓ An individual unit of information, such as an employee number or name, is called a **field**. A group of related fields is called a **record**. A collection of records is called a **file**. Sometimes **table**, **row**, and **column** are used in place of file, record, and field, respectively.
- ✓ In dBASE, each individual file (table) is called a **database file**. Thus, in dBASE, a database can actually be a collection of database files.
- ✓ **CHARACTER fields** may be used to store any printable character. **DATE fields** can only be used to store dates. **NUMERIC fields** can only be used to store numbers. Arithmetic operations can only be applied to numeric fields. **LOGICAL fields** consist of a single value representing a true or false condition. They can hold only T (True), F (False), Y (Yes), or N (No). **MEMO fields** can be used to store large blocks of text such as words or sentences.
- ✓ The **Control Center** is where you begin your work. It contains a list of files of various types in a box called the **work area**, as well as a collection of menus. (A **menu** is a list of actions from which you can choose.) The line at the bottom of the screen is called the **navigation line**. It indicates how special keys function.
- ✓ A **catalog** is a collection of related files. The files in the active catalog are the ones that are displayed at the Control Center.
- ✓ To use menus, press F10 to change to Menu mode. Use the LEFT and RIGHT ARROWs to move from one menu to another. Use the UP and DOWN ARROWs to move from one selection within a menu to another. When you have the choice you want highlighted, press ENTER.
- ✓ The **Dot Prompt mode** is a mode of operating with dBASE in which a single dot, called the **dot prompt** appears on the screen. To change from the Control Center to the Dot Prompt mode, select the "Exit to dot prompt" option of the Exit menu. To change from the Dot Prompt mode to the Control Center, press F2.
- ✓ To leave dBASE, select the "Quit to DOS" option of the Exit menu.
- ✓ To get help, use the F1 key.
- ✓ To change to a different catalog, use the "Use a different catalog" option of the Catalog menu, and then select the desired catalog. If the catalog does not yet exist, select <create> and then enter the name of the catalog.
- ✓ To create a database file, select <create> in the Data column and describe each of the fields that make up the database file. When done, select the "Exit" option of the Exit menu and indicate the name of the database file you have created. Use the "Change description of highlighted file" option of the Catalog menu to enter a description for the database file.

- ✓ To add or change records, press F2 at the Control Center. You then change to the Edit screen. You can then change back and forth between the Edit screen and the Browse screen by pressing F2. If the file contains no records, you will automatically be adding records. If the file contains records, you will be editing existing records. To add new ones, select the "Add new records" option of the Records menu.
- ✓ To move between records when entering or editing data, use the PAGE UP and PAGE DOWN keys if you are on the Edit screen.
- ✓ To print a report of all the data in your database file, press SHIFT-F9 (for Quick Report).
- ✓ A **backup copy** of a database file is a copy that is made and stored as a safety measure. If problems occur in the database file that is actively used, called the **live copy**, copying the backup version over the live version returns the database file to the state it was in when the backup was made.
- ✓ You can make a backup copy of a database file by using the DOS COPY command after you have exited dBASE. In the event of a problem, you can copy the backup copy over the live version by using a similar COPY command.
- ✓ To activate a database file, move the highlight to it, press ENTER, and then select "Use file."
- ✓ To access select data in a database, create a **query** by selecting <create> in the Queries column and then indicating the conditions that the records you want must satisfy. Optionally you can select to include only certain fields.
- ✓ The Query Design screen contains a **File skeleton** in which you indicate conditions and a **View skeleton** in which you indicate the list of fields that will appear in the results of the query. To move within a skeleton, press TAB to move to the right and SHIFT-TAB to move to the left. To move to the next skeleton, press F4. To move to the previous skeleton, press F3.
- ✓ To see the results of a query, press F2. In technical terms, you are **applying** the query.
- ✓ To print the results of a query, press SHIFT-F9 (for Quick Report).
- ✓ To change the View skeleton, place the highlight under the filename in the File skeleton and press F5 until the View skeleton disappears. Then, for each field you want in the View skeleton, move the highlight under the field name in the File skeleton and press F5.
- ✓ A **simple condition** consists of a single value and an operator in a single field. To enter a simple condition, type the condition and the operator in the appropriate column in the File skeleton.
- ✓ To enter a **compound condition** using AND, type the individual conditions on the same line. If they are in the same column, separate them with a comma.

- ✓ To enter a compound condition using OR, type the individual conditions on separate lines.
- ✓ To perform a summary calculation, place the appropriate **summary operator** in the appropriate column.
- ✓ To group data when performing summary calculations, place the words GROUP BY in the column that is to be used for **grouping**.

Review Questions

1. How do you load dBASE?
2. How do you select an option from a menu?
3. How do you escape from some task you have begun? Why might you want to do so?
4. How do you leave dBASE?
5. How do you get help on some specific option?
6. How do you create a database file? Describe the rules for naming a database file. How do you assign a field type? Describe the possible field types.
7. How do you activate a database file? Why must you do so?
8. Which option do you use to add records to a database file? How do you indicate that you are finished adding records?
9. How do you change records in a database file? How can you move to a record you need to change?
10. How do you delete records from a database file? When are records permanently removed from a database file?
11. How do you list records in a database file?
12. How do you make a backup copy? Why should you do so?
13. How do you restore a database file from a backup copy?
14. How do you display all the records in a database file?
15. How can you include only certain fields in a display?
16. How can you create a condition to limit the records included in a display?
17. How can you use a LOGICAL field in a condition?
18. How can you use a DATE field in a condition?
19. How can you find the records that contain a particular string of characters in some field?
20. How can you find records if you only know what the entry in some field is supposed to sound like?
21. How do you combine simple conditions with AND?
22. How do you combine simple conditions with OR?

23. How would you count the records in a database file that satisfy some condition?

24. How do you calculate a sum?

25. How do you calculate an average?

26. How do you group when calculating a sum or average? What does this mean?

CHECKPOINT EXERCISES

You are to create a database file to store information about a music library. The music is on cassette tape (CS), long-playing records (LP), or compact disk (CD), as indicated by the entry under the heading TYPE. A list of available music and field characteristics are as follows. The date field represents the date the music was obtained.

DATE	NAME	ARTIST	TYPE	COST	CATEGORY
02/22/92	Greatest Hits	Panache, Milo	LP	8.95	Classical
02/15/92	America	Judd, Mary	CS	5.95	Vocal
01/02/92	Rio Rio	Duran, Ralph	LP	8.95	Rock
02/15/92	Passione	Panache, Milo	LP	6.99	Classical
01/02/92	Country Hills	Lager, Ricky	CD	11.95	Country
02/22/92	Rockin'	Brady, Susan	CS	5.95	Rock
02/22/92	Pardners	Hudson, Randy	CS	5.95	Country
01/02/92	Private Love	Toner, Arlene	CD	11.95	Vocal
02/22/92	Moods	Silver, Sandy	CD	11.95	Rock

FIELD DESCRIPTION	FIELD NAME	FIELD TYPE	WIDTH	DECIMAL POSITIONS	INDEX
DATE	DATE	DATE	8		N
MUSIC NAME	NAME	CHARACTER	14		Y
ARTIST	ARTIST	CHARACTER	14		N
TYPE	TYPE	CHARACTER	2		N
COST	COST	NUMERIC	5	2	N
CATEGORY	CATEGORY	CHARACTER	9		N

Perform the following tasks:

1. Insert your data disk into drive A and then load dBASE.
2. Create a catalog called MUSICCAT.
3. Create the database file. Use the name MUSIC for the database file.
4. Enter the six fields in the preceding table.
5. Enter the preceding data. When you enter the third record, enter the name as Reeo Reeo, and the price as 9.85.
6. After you have entered the records, enter an additional record. You may make up whatever entries you want for the fields in this record.
7. After you have entered the records, enter an additional record. You may make up whatever entries you want for the fields in this record.

8. Use SHIFT-F9 to print a list of all the data.
9. Correct the third record by changing the name to Rio Rio and the price to 8.95.
10. Delete the extra record that you added. Permanently remove the record from the database file.
11. Use SHIFT-F9 to print a list of all the data.
12. Make a backup copy of this database file and corresponding production index file. Call them MUSICBCK.DBF and MUSICBCK.MDX, respectively.
13. Activate the database file so that it can be accessed.
14. Display all the fields and all the records.
15. Display the Name of the Music, Artist, Type, and Cost.
16. Display the music Category first and then the other fields in the record.
17. Display the records for the music of the Classical category.
18. Display the records for all music that costs $5.95.
19. Display the records for the music performed by an artist named Susan.
20. Display the records for all music whose name sounds like "Reo."
21. Display the records for all music on cassette tape (CS in Type).
22. Display the records for all music on compact disk (CD in type). Include the Type, Music Name, Artist, and Cost.
23. Display the records for all the music by the artist Milo Panache.
24. Display the records for all music that is of the Classical category and costs less than 8.95.
25. Display the records for all music that is of the Rock category and costs less than 8.95.
26. Display the Artist name and the Name of the music for all the Rock category that is unavailable on cassette tape.
27. Count the number of records in the database file.
28. Count the number of music selections in the Vocal category.
29. Sum the total cost of all types of music.
30. Sum the total cost of the music in the Country category.
31. Determine the average cost for types of music in the Country category.
32. Determine the average cost for types of music in each category.

Locating a Record

CONCEPTS

Before you can work on a record, you must be positioned on it. With small database files, you can usually find the records you want by pressing PAGE UP or PAGE DOWN while you are on the Edit screen. For large databases, this is very impractical. You would like to be able to easily locate a record just by knowing some condition that the record must satisfy.

Locating a Record That Satisfies a Condition

70

Remember that you can change the record pointer on the Edit screen by pressing PAGE UP (to move back to the previous record) and PAGE DOWN (to move to the next one). However, unless you only need to move a record or two, this method can be very cumbersome. It is quicker to use the Go To menu (Figure 8.1). The menu's first option, "Top record," moves you directly to the first record in the database file. The next option, "Last record," moves you to the last record. If you pick the third option, "Record number," dBASE asks you for the number of the record to which you wish to move. When you enter the number you want, you are taken directly to that record.

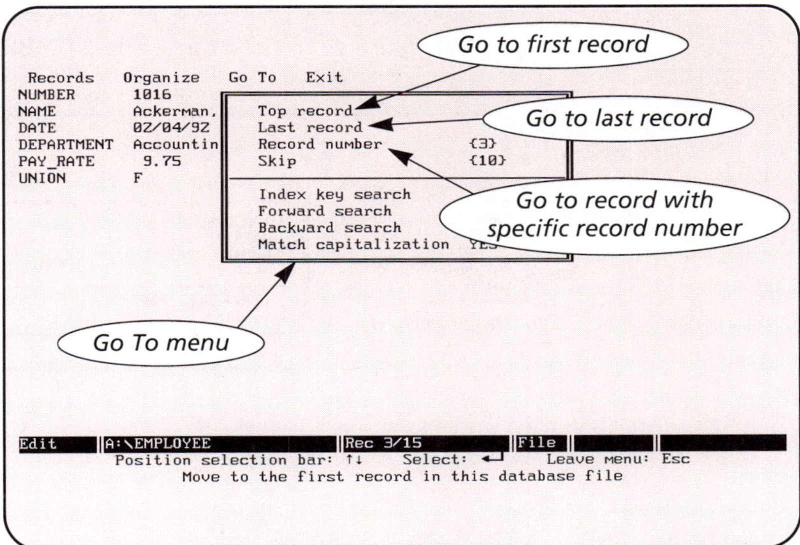

Figure 8.1
Edit Screen

What if you don't know the record number of the record you want? What if you only know something about the record? For example, suppose you want to make some change to the data for employee 1016, but you don't know where this employee is located in the file. This is where the "Forward search" option can be very helpful. It allows you to locate a record on the basis of some condition.

Finding the Next Record That Satisfies a Condition 70

In some cases, you may not want the first record meeting a condition. You may want the second or the third or the tenth. For example, you may want to find the second employee in the Accounting department or you may want to step through all employees in the Accounting department, one after the other. To do so, you use the "Forward search" option to find the first one. After you have done that, you can use the same "Forward search" option to find the next one.

TUTORIAL

In this tutorial, you use the "Forward search" option to find records that satisfy certain conditions.

1 Locate the employee whose number is 1016.

Activate	EMPLOYEE	
Press	F2 once or twice, as required	Moves to Edit screen.

Make sure your cursor is in the NUMBER field.

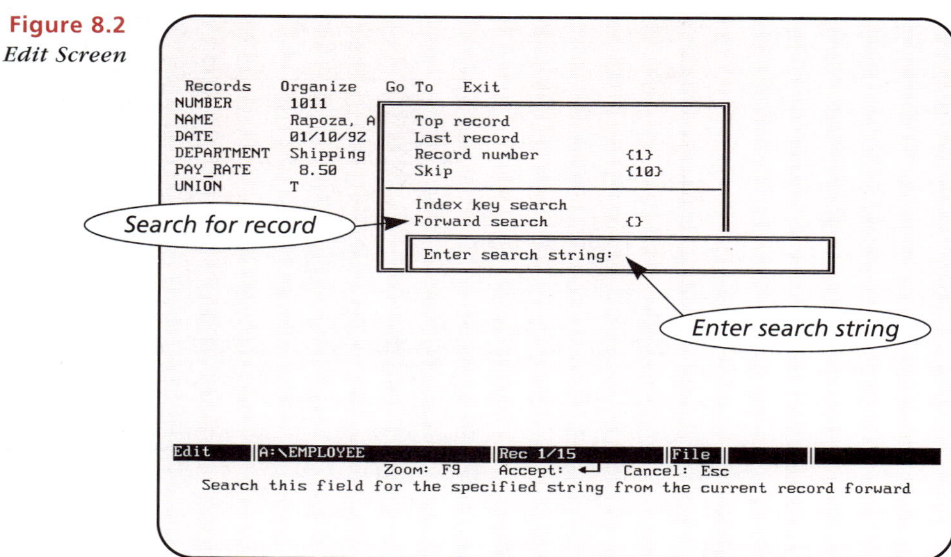

Figure 8.2
Edit Screen

Figure 8.3
Edit Screen

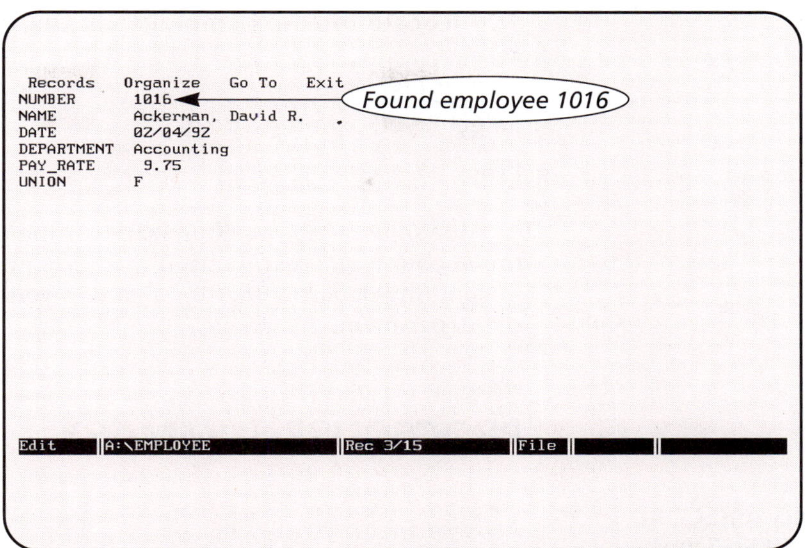

> **TIP** When you pick "Forward Search," you are asking dBASE to search starting with the current record and move forward until it finds the next record matching the search string. To be sure you find the first such record, play it safe by using the "Top record" option to move to the *first* record before you do the forward search.

Select	"Forward search"	from Go To menu.

You are then asked to enter a *search string*, that is, the particular value you are looking for (Figure 8.2).

Type	1016	
Press	↵ ENTER	Completes search string.

dBASE then locates this employee for you (Figure 8.3). You may wonder how dBASE knew that you wanted to search for a record on which the value of NUMBER was 1016. Why didn't dBASE search the NAME, PAY_RATE, or some other field? dBASE searches only the field in which the cursor is currently positioned. That is why you were instructed to make sure the cursor was in the NUMBER field before beginning your search. ◀

2 Locate the first employee in the Accounting department.
Make sure you are at the beginning of the EMPLOYEE database file. (If not, select the "Top record" option of the Go To menu.)

Press	↓ three times	Moves to DEPARTMENT field.
Select	"Forward search"	from Go To menu.
Press	←BACKSPACE	Erases previous entry.
Type	Accounting	
Press	↵ ENTER	Completes search string.

dBASE then locates the first employee in the Accounting department.

3 Locate the next employee in the Accounting department.

Select	"Forward search"	from Go To menu.
Press	↵ ENTER	

dBASE uses the previous search string to locate the next employee in the Accounting department. If there are no more employees in the Accounting department, dBASE moves you back to the first employee in the department.

PROCEDURE SUMMARY

LOCATING A RECORD THAT SATISFIES A CONDITION

Activate the database file.	
Move to the Edit screen.	F2
Move the cursor to the field you wish to search.	↓
Select the "Forward search" option of the Go To menu.	
Enter the value for which you wish to search.	(your input) ↵ ENTER

FINDING THE NEXT RECORD THAT SATISFIES A CONDITION

Select the "Forward search" option of the Go To menu.	
Do not change the condition.	↵ ENTER

EXERCISES

1. Use the CHECK database file and the "Forward search" option to find the check whose number is 110.
2. Use the "Forward search" option to find the first check in the CHECK database file written for Food.
3. Use the appropriate option to locate the next check written for Food.

Using the Browse Screen

> **TIP** Remember that you can move from the Edit screen to the Browse screen by pressing F2. You can also move from the Browse screen to the Edit screen by pressing F2. Thus it is very easy to move between these two screens.

CONCEPTS You can add, change, and delete records using the Edit screen. On the Edit screen, you see one record at a time. Sometimes you might prefer to see several records at a time, presented in the form of a list.

Using the Browse Screen to Update Records 72

To edit data in list form, use the Browse screen rather than the Edit screen. The Browse screen displays up to 17 records on the screen at one time and as many fields as will fit horizontally on the screen (Figure 9.1).

The current active record is highlighted. You can move the highlight to any other record by pressing the DOWN ARROW or UP ARROW (which moves one record), PAGE DOWN or PAGE UP (which moves one screenful), or by using the Go To menu. Once you have moved to the record to be changed, you then move the cursor to the field to be changed. You can move the cursor one field to the right by pressing the TAB key and one field to the left by pressing SHIFT-TAB. You can then make the change.

Figure 9.1
Browse Screen

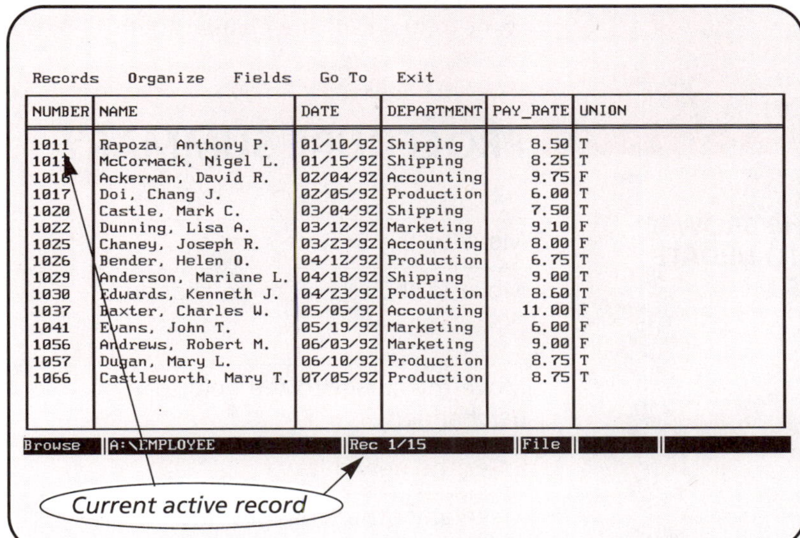

Records Organize Fields Go To Exit

NUMBER	NAME	DATE	DEPARTMENT	PAY_RATE	UNION
1011	Rapoza, Anthony P.	01/10/92	Shipping	8.50	T
1013	McCormack, Nigel L.	01/15/92	Shipping	8.25	T
1016	Ackerman, David R.	02/04/92	Accounting	9.75	F
1017	Doi, Chang J.	02/05/92	Production	6.00	T
1020	Castle, Mark C.	03/04/92	Shipping	7.50	T
1022	Dunning, Lisa A.	03/12/92	Marketing	9.10	F
1025	Chaney, Joseph R.	03/23/92	Accounting	8.00	F
1026	Bender, Helen O.	04/12/92	Production	6.75	T
1029	Anderson, Mariane L.	04/18/92	Shipping	9.00	T
1030	Edwards, Kenneth J.	04/23/92	Production	8.60	T
1037	Baxter, Charles W.	05/05/92	Accounting	11.00	F
1041	Evans, John T.	05/19/92	Marketing	6.00	F
1056	Andrews, Robert M.	06/03/92	Marketing	9.00	F
1057	Dugan, Mary L.	06/10/92	Production	8.75	T
1066	Castleworth, Mary T.	07/05/92	Production	8.75	T

Browse | A:\EMPLOYEE | Rec 1/15 | File

You can also use the Browse screen to add records to a file. Just move the reverse video block past the last record. The message "Add new record? (Y/N)" appears on the screen. If you enter a Y, spaces are displayed at the bottom of the screen so that you can enter a new record. If you enter an N, the highlight remains on the bottom row. The most common method of adding records, however, is to use the Edit screen, as you saw earlier.

TUTORIAL

In this tutorial, you use the Browse screen to update records.

1 Change Helen Bender's pay rate to $7.00.

Activate	EMPLOYEE	
Press	F2 once or twice	Moves to Browse screen.
Press	↓ seven times	Moves to Helen Bender's record.
Press	TAB four times	Moves to PAY_RATE.
Type	7.00	Changes pay rate.
Select	"Exit"	from Exit menu.

The change is then saved, and you are returned to the Control Center. If you needed to make changes to several records, you would probably want to make all the changes before exiting.

PROCEDURE SUMMARY

USING THE BROWSE SCREEN TO UPDATE RECORDS

Move to the Browse screen.	F2
Move to the record to be changed.	↑ or ↓ or PAGE UP or PAGE DOWN
Move the cursor to the field to be changed.	TAB or SHIFT-TAB
Enter the new data	(your input)
Make any other changes in the same manner.	(your input)
Select the "Exit" option of the Exit menu.	

EXERCISES

1. Use the Browse screen to change the amount for check 102 to $95.00.
2. Use the Browse screen to change the payee for check 108 to Amble Inn. In addition, change the amount to $25.00 and change TAXDED to false.
3. List all the records in the CHECK database file.

TOPIC 10

Using Conditions to Change Records

CONCEPTS

The Edit and Browse screens allow you to make changes to the data in a database file by moving to the appropriate field in the appropriate record and then typing the new data. In some cases, you might need to make the same change to all the records that satisfy some condition. It would be very cumbersome to use the Edit or Browse screen and make all these changes individually. It would be far more convenient to specify a condition that identifies the record or records to be changed and then simply indicate the new values.

Using Update Queries

78

Fortunately, by using a special kind of query, called an **update query**, you can update a database file in this fashion. To illustrate the benefits to this approach, suppose you needed to give each employee in the Marketing department a 50-cent raise. To do so using the Edit screen or the Browse screen, you would need to move through the entire EMPLOYEE database file. Whenever you came to an employee with the value "Marketing" in the DEPARTMENT field, you would need to move the cursor to the PAY_RATE field, calculate what the new pay rate should be, and then type the new value. By contrast, with update queries, you only need to enter a condition that identifies the records to be updated and then enter the replacement value.

The replacement value you enter can be a specific number (like 6.75) or an expression (like PAY_RATE + .50). Such expressions can involve + (addition), - (subtraction), * (multiplication), or / (division).

TUTORIAL

In this tutorial, you use an update query to change all the records that satisfy some condition.

1 Use a condition to change the pay rate of employee 1026 (Helen Bender) from 7.00 back to 6.75. This reverses the change you made earlier.

Activate	EMPLOYEE	
Select	<create>	in Queries column.

You should now see the Query Design screen.

Select	"Specify update operation"	from Update menu.

You then see a list of possible update operations (Figure 10.1).

Select	"Replace values in Employee.dbf"

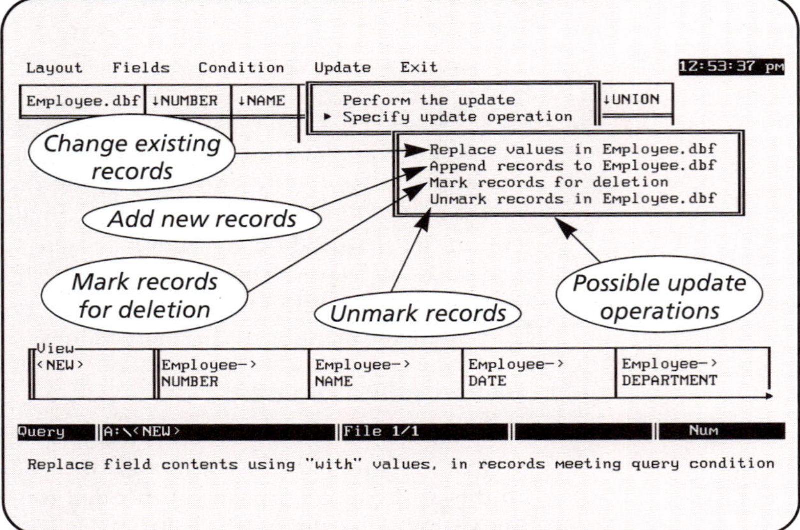

Figure 10.1
Query Design Screen

You are then asked if you wish to proceed or cancel the request. As the message in the box points out, if you proceed with the update query, the View skeleton is deleted. This is not a problem because it is the File skeleton that you use to specify the update.

Select	"Proceed"	Proceeds with update query.

Your screen then looks like Figure 10.2. The word "Target" above Employee.dbf indicates that this database file is the *target* of the update. The word "Replace" that appears underneath Employee.dbf indicates that the update operation is *replacing* existing data. You now need to enter a condition and a replacement expression.

Press	TAB	Moves to NUMBER column.
Type	"1026"	
Press	↵ ENTER	Completes condition.

Unlike the searches on the Go To menu, when you use the Query Design screen, values for character fields must be enclosed in quotes.

Figure 10.2
Query Design Screen

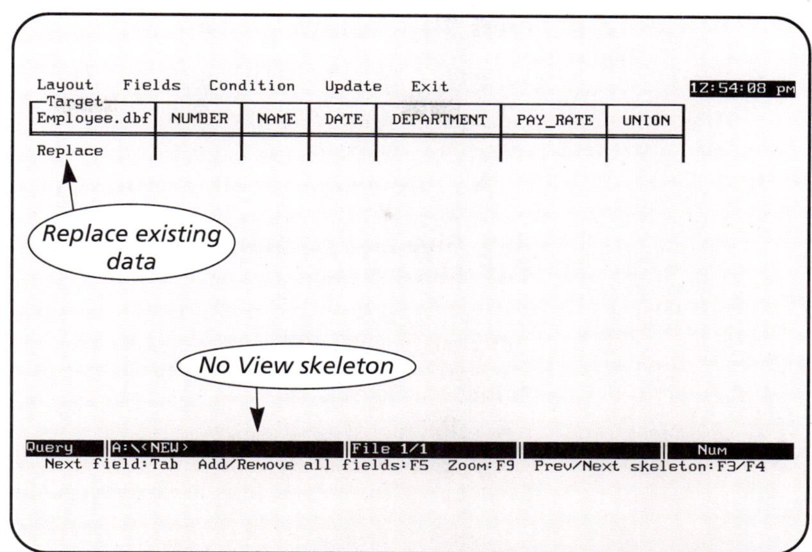

Press	TAB four times	Moves to PAY_RATE column.
Type	WITH 6.75	
Press	↵ ENTER	Completes replacement expression.
Select	"Perform the update"	from Update menu.

Your update is made, and you should see the screen shown in Figure 10.3. Note that the screen shows how many records were replaced, in this case, only 1. As indicated on the screen, you can press F2 to see the results of the update. If you do not need to see the results, simply press any other key.

Figure 10.3
Query Design Screen

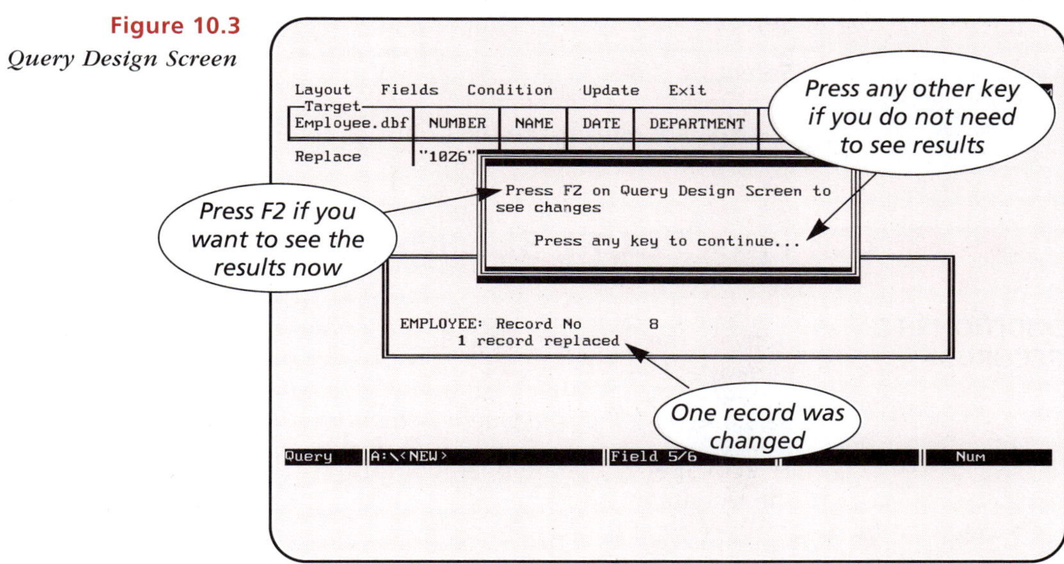

Press	(any key)	
Select	"Abandon changes and exit"	from Exit menu.
Select	"Yes"	Abandons query.

You are returned to the Control Center.

2 Give all Marketing department employees a 50-cent raise.

Activate	EMPLOYEE	unless already active.
Select	<create>	in Queries column.
Select	"Specify update operation"	from Update menu.
Select	"Replace values in Employee.dbf"	
Select	"Proceed"	Proceeds with update query.
Press	TAB four times	Moves to DEPARTMENT column.
Type	"Marketing"	
Press	↵ ENTER	Completes condition.
Press	TAB	Moves to PAY_RATE column.
Type	WITH PAY_RATE + .50	
Press	↵ ENTER	Completes replacement expression.
Select	"Perform the update"	from Update menu.
Press	(any key)	
Select	"Abandon changes and exit"	from Exit menu.
Select	"Yes"	Abandons query.

You are returned to the Control Center.

PROCEDURE SUMMARY

USING CONDITIONS TO UPDATE RECORDS

Activate the database file unless it is already active.

Select <create> in the Queries column.

Select "Specify update operation" from the Update menu.

Select "Replace values in ..."	
Select "Proceed."	
Enter the condition.	(your input)
Enter the replacement expression.	(your input)
Select "Perform the update" from the Update menu.	
Press any key.	(your input)
Select "Abandon changes and exit" from the Exit menu.	
Select "Yes."	

EXERCISES

1. Use an update query to subtract $0.50 from the pay rate of all employees in the EMPLOYEE database who are in the Marketing department.
2. Use an update query to change the check amount on check 105 in the CHECKS database to $24.75.
3. Use an update query to add $1.00 to the amount of all checks written to Sav-Mor Groceries.
4. List all the records in the CHECK database file.

Deleting Records

CONCEPTS

It is sometimes necessary to delete records from a file. For example, if an employee no longer works for the company, the employee's record should be removed (deleted) from the EMPLOYEE file. You have already seen how to delete records using the Edit screen by moving to the record to be marked and then pressing CONTROL-U. You can delete records on the Browse screen in exactly the same way.

When you delete records from a database file using either of these options, the records are not actually removed from the file at that time. Instead, dBASE merely marks them as being deleted. You must use the "Erase marked records" option of the Organize menu to physically remove these records from the file. Until you do so, the records are still in the file. dBASE, however, indicates which records have been marked. When records are being edited and the current active record happens to be one that has been marked for deletion, the letters "Del" appear near the right-hand end of the status line.

Using Conditions to Mark Records for Deletion

83

> **TIP** Always be very careful when you mark and permanently remove marked records. Otherwise, you could lose critical information.

Sometimes you need to delete all the records that satisfy a certain condition. For example, if you had a database file of orders placed by the customers of your organization, you would periodically want to delete all the orders that had been paid (that is, all orders on which the balance owed was zero). This process would certainly be cumbersome using the Edit or the Browse screen. Fortunately you can use an update query to mark all the records that satisfy certain conditions. When you have marked all the records you want to delete, you can then select the appropriate option to permanently remove the marked records. ◀

Using Conditions to Unmark Records

84

Just as it is useful to have an option to mark all the records that satisfy a certain condition, it is also useful to have an option to unmark such records. This is especially important if you inadvertently create the wrong condition when you marked the records. You need an easy way to unmark them. Fortunately you can use an update query to unmark all records satisfying certain conditions. Then such records will no longer be marked for deletion.

TUTORIAL In this tutorial, you use an update query to mark all the records that satisfy some condition for deletion. You also use an update query to unmark records.

1 Use the "Delete" option to mark the employee whose name is Robert M. Andrews for deletion.

Activate	EMPLOYEE	
Select	<create>	in Queries column.

You should now see the Query Design screen.

Select	"Specify update operation"	from Update menu.
Select	"Mark records for deletion"	
Select	"Proceed"	Proceeds with update query.
Press	TAB twice	Moves to NAME column.
Type	"Andrews, Robert M."	
Press	↵ ENTER	Completes condition.
Select	"Perform the update"	from Update menu.
Press	Y	
Press	↵ ENTER	

Marks record for deletion.

Press	(any key)	
Select	"Abandon changes and exit"	from Exit menu.
Select	"Yes"	Abandons query.

You are returned to the Control Center. Normally, if you only have a single record to delete, you can use either the Edit or Browse screen. If you need to delete all the records that satisfy a certain condition (such as all the employees in a given department), update queries are ideal.

2 Use the "Recall" option to unmark the record on which the employee name is Robert M. Andrews.

Activate	EMPLOYEE	
Select	<create>	in Queries column.

You should now see the Query Design screen.

Select	"Specify update operation"	from Update menu.
Select	"Unmark records"	
Select	"Proceed"	Proceeds with update query.
Press	(TAB) twice	Moves to NAME column.
Type	"Andrews, Robert M."	
Press	(↵ ENTER)	Completes condition.
Select	"Perform the update"	from Update menu.

The record for Robert Andrews is then unmarked.

Press	(any key)	
Select	"Abandon changes and exit"	from Exit menu.
Select	"Yes"	Abandons query.

You are returned to the Control Center.

PROCEDURE SUMMARY

USING CONDITIONS TO MARK RECORDS FOR DELETION

Activate the database file unless it is already active.	
Select <create> in the Queries column.	
Select "Specify update operation" from the Update menu.	
Select "Mark records for deletion."	
Select "Proceed."	
Enter the condition.	(your input)
Select "Perform the update" from the Update menu.	
Press any key.	(your input)
Select "Abandon changes and exit" from the Exit menu.	
Select "Yes."	

USING CONDITIONS TO UNMARK RECORDS

Activate the database file unless it is already active.	
Select <create> in the Queries column.	
Select "Specify update operation" from the Update menu.	
Select "Unmark records."	
Select "Proceed."	
Enter the condition.	(your input)
Select "Perform the update" from the Update menu.	
Press any key.	(your input)
Select "Abandon changes and exit" from the Exit menu.	
Select "Yes."	

EXERCISES

1. Use an update query to mark all checks written to Sav-Mor Groceries for deletion.
2. Use an update query to unmark all checks written to Sav-Mor Groceries.
3. Use the Edit screen to mark check 111 for deletion.
4. Use the Browse screen to mark check 110 for deletion.
5. Physically remove the marked records from the CHECK database file.
6. List all the records in the CHECK database file.

Creating and Using a Custom Form

CONCEPTS

You have already used the Edit screen to add new records to a database file and to change existing records. When you did, you used a form on the screen to enter data. Although the form did provide you with some assistance in the task, the form was not particularly attractive or helpful. The fields were simply stacked on top of each other. The names shown on the screen were the names of the fields, which are not as descriptive as they might be.

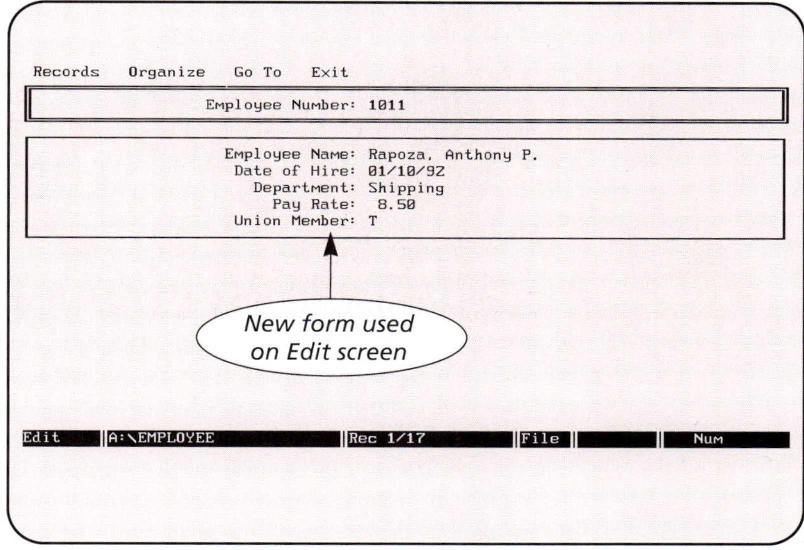

Figure 12.1
Edit Screen

In this section, you see how to create custom screen forms like the one shown in Figure 12.1. Notice that the names that appear in front of the fields (often called **prompts** since they *prompt* the user to enter a particular item of data) are more descriptive and that the prompts and fields are located near the center of the screen.

Creating an Initial Form 93

The simplest way to begin creating a custom screen form is to let dBASE create an initial form for you. To do so, you use a special option called "Quick layout." This option creates an initial form that looks exactly like the one you normally see when you use the Edit screen. You then modify this screen form, gradually transforming it into the one you want.

Adding Blank Lines 93

One way to improve the appearance of a form is to add blank lines. This helps related fields to be seen together and unrelated fields to be separated.

Changing the Prompts 93

Making the prompts more descriptive is another way to improve a form. The prompt "Employee number:" is more descriptive, for example, than "NUMBER." The user has a clearer idea of what to enter.

Repositioning Fields and Prompts 93

Often a form looks better if the contents are approximately centered on the screen. This requires repositioning the fields and prompts.

Adding Boxes 94

Boxes can often improve the look of a form. For example, you could place a double box around the primary key to emphasize its special nature. (The **primary key** is the field that uniquely identifies a record. The employee number field, for example, in the EMPLOYEE database file is the primary key since no two employees can have the same number.) You could then place a single box around the remainder of the fields. All of these features combine to give the form a much more pleasing appearance.

Saving a Form 94

When you have completed the design of the form, you need to save your work. If, by some chance, you do not like the form you have created, you can instead abandon your work. If you choose this option, all your work will be lost. You could then begin designing the form again from scratch.

Using a Form 94

To use a form you have created, you must first activate the database file. Then you must also activate the form. Once the form is active, it will appear on the screen whenever you use the Edit screen.

Modifying a Form 94

You can modify a form design at any time. You make any changes to the design in the same way you did when you created the design in the first place. When you have finished, save your work and the changes will be made.

TUTORIAL In this tutorial, you create a custom form. You then use the form to update records.

1 **Create an initial form.** Begin creating the form shown in Figure 12.1.

Activate	EMPLOYEE	
Select	<create>	in Forms column.
Select	"Quick layout"	from Layout menu.

At this point, dBASE creates the form shown in Figure 12.2. It is precisely the form you normally see on the Edit screen. The 9s and Xs represent the fields.) You now modify this form, gradually turning it into precisely what you want.

Figure 12.2
Forms Design Screen

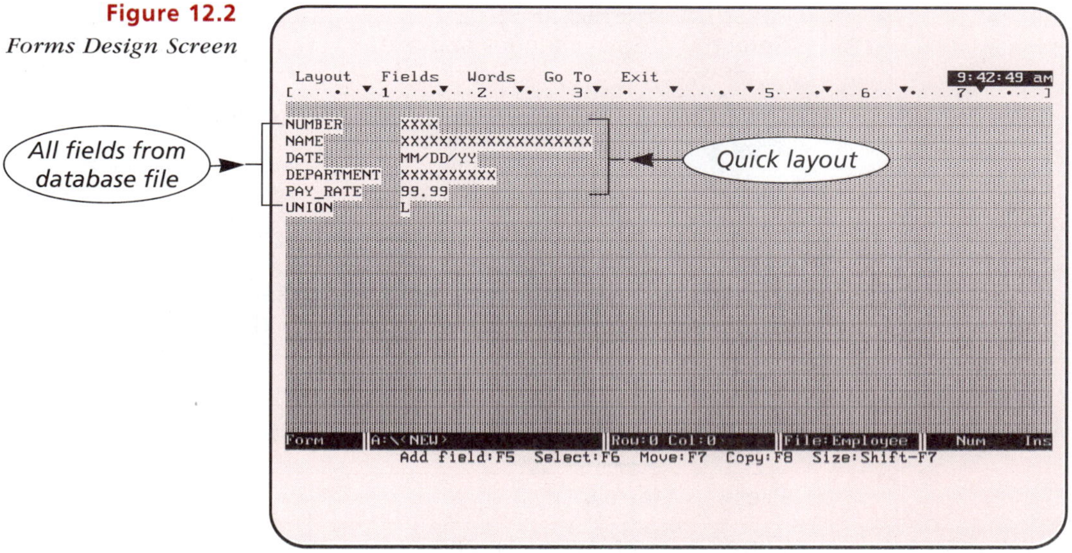

```
 Layout   Fields   Words   Go To   Exit                              9:42:49 am
NUMBER      XXXX
NAME        XXXXXXXXXXXXXXXXXXXX
DATE        MM/DD/YY
DEPARTMENT  XXXXXXXXXX
PAY_RATE    99.99
UNION       L
Form    A:\<NEW>        Row:0 Col:0      File:Employee        Num   Ins
             Add field:F5  Select:F6  Move:F7  Copy:F8  Size:Shift-F7
```

All fields from database file

Quick layout

2 **Save the form.** Call the form EMPLOYEE. This name emphasizes that it is a form for the EMPLOYEE database.

Select	"Save changes and exit"	from Exit menu.
Type	EMPLOYEE	Names the form.

You may wonder if giving a database file the same name as a form could cause a problem. After all, both files are stored on your disk and all the files stored on a disk must have unique names. Fortunately this is not a problem because the files are of different types, and consequently dBASE assigns them different extensions. Thus, as far as DOS is concerned, they have different names. When you return to the Control Center, you will see your form in the Forms column.

3 Modify the EMPLOYEE form by adding blank lines.

Activate	EMPLOYEE	unless already active.
Select	EMPLOYEE	in Forms column.
Select	"Modify Layout"	
Press	CTRL-N	Adds extra blank line at beginning.

You now add two blank lines between the first line (NUMBER in the figure) and the second (NAME). Feel free to add any other blank lines that you think enhance the look of your form.

Press	↓ repeatedly	Moves cursor to N of NAME.
Press	CTRL-N twice	
Select	"Save changes and exit"	from Exit menu.

4 Change the prompts on the EMPLOYEE form.

Activate	EMPLOYEE	unless already active.
Select	EMPLOYEE	in Forms column.
Select	"Modify Layout"	

You must be in Insert mode.

Press	INSERT	Puts you in Insert mode.
Press	(arrow keys)	Moves cursor to N of NUMBER.
Type	Employee Number:	Creates new prompt.
Press	CTRL-T	Removes old prompt.
Press	(arrow keys)	Moves cursor to N of NAME.
Type	Employee Name:	Creates new prompt.
Press	CTRL-T	Removes old prompt.
Press	(arrow keys)	Moves cursor to D of DATE.
Type	Date of Hire:	Creates new prompt.
Press	CTRL-T	Removes old prompt.
Press	(arrow keys)	Moves cursor to D of DEPARTMENT.

Type	Department:	Creates new prompt.
Press	CTRL-T	Removes old prompt.
Press	(arrow keys)	Moves cursor to P of PAY_RATE.
Type	Pay Rate:	Creates new prompt.
Press	CTRL-T	Removes old prompt.
Press	(arrow keys)	Moves cursor to U of UNION.
Type	Union Member:	Creates new prompt.
Press	CTRL-T	Removes old prompt.
Select	"Save changes and exit"	from Exit menu.

5 Move the fields on the EMPLOYEE form.

Activate	EMPLOYEE	unless already active.
Select	EMPLOYEE	in Forms column.
Select	"Modify Layout"	

To move a field on a form, you first need to select it. You do so by moving the cursor into the field, pressing F6, and then pressing Enter. Once you have selected it, you move it by pressing F7, moving the cursor to the new location, and then pressing Enter.

Press	(arrow keys)	Moves cursor into NUMBER field.
Press	F6, ↵ENTER	Selects field.
Press	F7, → 20 times, ↵ENTER	Moves field.
Press	(arrow keys)	Moves cursor into NAME field.
Press	F6, ↵ENTER	Selects field.
Press	F7, → 22 times, ↵ENTER	Moves field.
Press	(arrow keys)	Moves cursor into DATE field.
Press	F6, ↵ENTER	Selects field.
Press	F7, → 23 times, ↵ENTER	Moves field.
Press	(arrow keys)	Moves cursor into DEPARTMENT field.
Press	F6, ↵ENTER	Selects field.
Press	F7, → 25 times, ↵ENTER	Moves field.

Press	(arrow keys)	Moves cursor into PAY_RATE field.
Press	F6, ↵ENTER	Selects field.
Press	F7, → 27 times, ↵ENTER	Moves field.
Press	(arrow keys)	Moves cursor into UNION field.
Press	F6, ↵ENTER	Selects field.
Press	F7, → 23 times, ↵ENTER	Moves field.

Your form should now look like the one shown in Figure 12.3.

Figure 12.3
Forms Design Screen

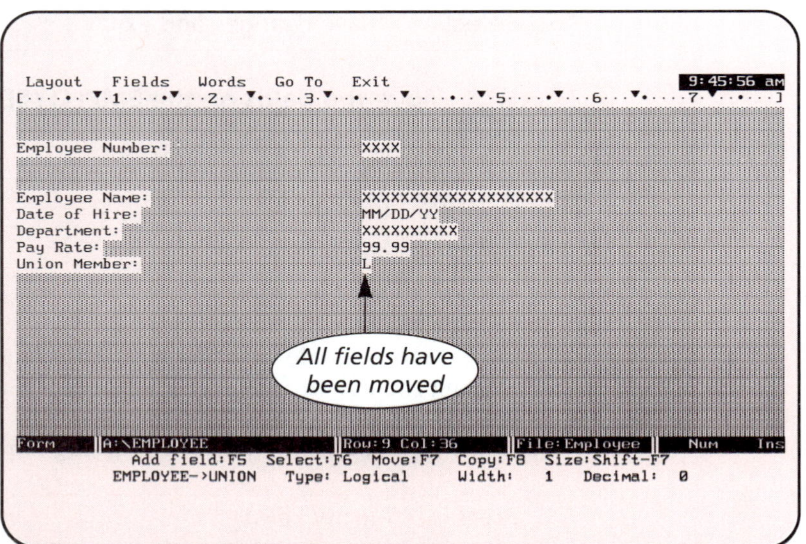

Select	"Save changes and exit"	from Exit menu.

6 Move the prompts on the EMPLOYEE form.

Activate	EMPLOYEE	unless already active.
Select	EMPLOYEE	in Forms column.
Select	"Modify Layout"	

To move a string of characters, like a prompt, you first need to select it. Move the cursor to the first character, press F6, move the cursor to the last character, and then press Enter. Then you can move the string by pressing F7, moving the cursor to the new location, and pressing Enter.

Press	(arrow keys)	Moves cursor to E in Employee Number.
Press	F6, → 15 times, ↵ENTER	Selects prompt.
Press	F7, → 4 times, ↵ENTER	Moves prompt.
Press	(arrow keys)	Moves cursor to E in Employee Name.
Press	F6, → 13 times, ↵ENTER	Selects prompt.
Press	F7, → 8 times, ↵ENTER	Moves prompt.
Press	(arrow keys)	Moves cursor to D in Date of Hire.
Press	F6, → 12 times, ↵ENTER	Selects prompt.
Press	F7, → 10 times, ↵ENTER	Moves prompt.
Press	(arrow keys)	Moves cursor to D in Department.
Press	F6, → 10 times, ↵ENTER	Selects prompt.
Press	F7, → 14 times, ↵ENTER	Moves prompt.
Press	(arrow keys)	Moves cursor to P in Pay Rate.
Press	F6, → 8 times, ↵ENTER	Selects prompt.
Press	F7, → 18 times, ↵ENTER	Moves prompt.
Press	(arrow keys)	Moves cursor to U in Union Member.
Press	F6, → 12 times, ↵ENTER	Selects prompt.
Press	F7, → 10 times, ↵ENTER	Moves prompt.
Select	"Save changes and exit"	from Exit menu.

7 Add boxes to the EMPLOYEE form.

Activate	EMPLOYEE	unless already active.
Select	EMPLOYEE	in Forms column.
Select	"Modify Layout"	
Select	"Box"	from Layout menu.
Select	"Double line"	

> **TIP** If you happen to put the box in the wrong place or make it the wrong size, you can move or resize the box. The process, however, is more trouble than it's worth. The easiest way to correct the problem is to move the cursor anywhere in the border of the box (the double line) and select it (press F6, ENTER). Then press DEL to delete the box. Then create a brand new box by following the same steps you used before.

Press	(arrow keys)	Moves cursor to beginning of line above line containing "Employee Number."
Press	↵ ENTER	
Press	(arrow keys)	Moves cursor to end of line below line containing "Employee Number."
Press	↵ ENTER	Causes double box to appear. ◀
Select	"Box"	from Layout menu.
Select	"Single line"	
Press	(arrow keys)	Moves cursor to first position on line above Employee Name.
Press	↵ ENTER	
Press	(arrow keys)	Moves cursor to last position on line below Union member.
Press	↵ ENTER	Causes single box to appear.

See the previous tip if you made a mistake.

Select	"Save changes and exit"	from Exit menu.

8 **Activate and use the form you created.** Before you activate a form, your database file must be active. In this case, it is active because you activated it in the previous task. If it were not, you would have to activate it *before* activating the form.

Activate	EMPLOYEE	unless already active.
Select	"EMPLOYEE"	in Forms column.
Select	"Display data"	

The normal dBASE form is replaced with your own custom form (Figure 12.1). Notice that the form shown on the screen is precisely the one you created. Other than the new form, there is no difference in the use of the Edit screen. You can still use it to add records and to make changes exactly as you did before. You can still press PgDn to move to the next record. You can still use the Go To menu to find records. You will just see a different form on the screen, one that has a nicer appearance. When you are done using the form, return to the Control Center.

Select	"Exit"	from Exit menu.

PROCEDURE SUMMARY

CREATING AN INITIAL FORM

Activate the database file.	(your choice)
Select <create> in the Forms column.	
Select "Quick layout" from the Layout menu.	

ADDING BLANK LINES

Move the cursor to the beginning of the line where you want to insert a blank line.	(arrow keys)
Insert blank line.	CTRL-N

CHANGING THE PROMPTS

Make sure that "Ins" appears in the lower right-hand corner of your screen.	INSERT
Move the cursor to the first letter in the prompt that is to be changed.	(arrow keys)
Type the new prompt.	(your input), CTRL-T

REPOSITIONING FIELDS AND PROMPTS

To select a field:

Move the cursor into the field.	(arrow keys)
Select the field.	F6, ↵ ENTER

To select a prompt (or other character string):

Move the cursor to the first position in the prompt.	(arrow keys)
Begin selecting the prompt.	F6
Move the cursor to the last position in the prompt.	(arrow keys)
Complete selection.	↵ ENTER

To move a field or prompt:

Select the field or prompt.	(your choice)
Begin moving the field or prompt.	F7

Move the cursor to the new position.	(arrow keys)
Complete the move.	↵ ENTER
If the new position would result in covering a previous position (that is, the new and old positions overlap), you are asked if it is all right to "Delete covered field or text." Assuming that it is, answer "Yes."	Y

ADDING BOXES

Select "Box" from the Layout menu.	
Select "Double line" (for a double box) or "Single line" (for a single box).	(your choice)
Move the cursor to the upper left-hand corner of the box.	(arrow keys)
Select the upper left-hand corner.	↵ ENTER
Move the cursor to the lower right-hand corner of the box.	(arrow keys)
Select the lower right-hand corner.	↵ ENTER

SAVING A FORM

Select "Save changes and exit" from the Exit menu.	
If it is the first time you have saved your form, type the name of the form.	(your input)

USING A FORM

Activate the database file.	(your choice)
Select the form in the Forms column.	(your choice)
Select "Display data."	

MODIFYING A FORM

Activate the database file.	(your choice)
Select the form in the Forms column.	(your choice)
Select "Modify Layout."	
Make any changes you wish to make.	
Save the form.	

EXERCISES

1. Create a form for the CHECK database file that is similar to the form you created for the EMPLOYEE database file. Call it CKFORM.
2. Activate this form. Select the Edit screen to make sure that the form is active. (Select the "Exit" option of the Exit menu to leave the Edit screen option once you have seen your form on the screen.)

Sorting a Database File

CONCEPTS

Sometimes you would like to see the data in a database file in a particular order. It may be helpful, for example, to see the employees listed alphabetically by name. In another case, it might be better to see them in order of employee number, or, perhaps, in order of pay rate. In still another, you might prefer to see them in order of department, so that all the employees in the Accounting department appear first, then the employees in Marketing, and so on. You can accomplish this by sorting the database file. **Sorting** a database file means rearranging the records on the basis of the values in some field or combination of fields. Such fields are called **sort keys**.

In dBASE, when you sort, you create a brand new file. The new file contains the same records as the original. The only difference is that the records have been rearranged in the desired order.

Sorting a Database File on a Single Field (103)

To illustrate the process, suppose the data in the EMPLOYEE file is sorted by name. In other words, NAME is the sort key. (CHARACTER, NUMERIC, and DATE fields can be sorted. LOGICAL and MEMO fields cannot be sorted. Because NAME is a CHARACTER field, there is no problem using it as the key field.) The results of sorting the employees by name are shown in Figure 13.1.

Figure 13.1
Employee Records Sorted by Name

Record#	NUMBER	NAME	DATE	DEPARTMENT	PAY_RATE	UNION
1	1016	Ackerman, David R.	02/04/92	Accounting	9.75	.F.
2	1029	Anderson, Mariane L.	04/18/92	Shipping	9.00	.T.
3	1056	Andrews, Robert M.	06/03/92	Marketing	9.00	.F.
4	1037	Baxter, Charles W.	05/05/92	Accounting	11.00	.F.
5	1026	Bender, Helen O.	04/12/92	Production	6.75	.T.
6	1066	Castleworth, Mary T.	07/05/92	Production	8.75	.T.
7	1020	Castle, Mark C.	03/04/92	Shipping	7.50	.T.
8	1025	Chaney, Joseph R.	03/23/92	Accounting	8.00	.F.
9	1017	Doi, Chan J.	02/05/92	Production	6.00	.T.
10	1057	Dugan, Mary L.	06/10/92	Production	8.75	.T.
11	1022	Dunning, Lisa A.	03/12/92	Marketing	9.10	.F.
12	1030	Edwards, Kenneth J.	04/23/92	Production	8.60	.T.
13	1047	Evans, John T.	05/19/92	Marketing	6.00	.F.
14	1013	McCormack, Nigel L.	01/15/92	Shipping	8.25	.T.
15	1011	Rapoza, Anthony P.	01/10/92	Shipping	8.50	.T.

Using a Sorted File (104)

When you sort a database file, you produce another database file that contains the sorted data. The original, unsorted file is still active, however. Thus, in order to use a sorted database file, you must activate it. Once you have done so, you have the data in the order you want.

Sorting on More Than One Field (104)

Sometimes you need to sort on more than one field. For example, you might want the employees sorted by department *and* all the employees in a given department sorted by name. In this case, you would have two sort keys, DEPARTMENT and NAME. Figure 13.2 illustrates the employee records sorted by name within department.

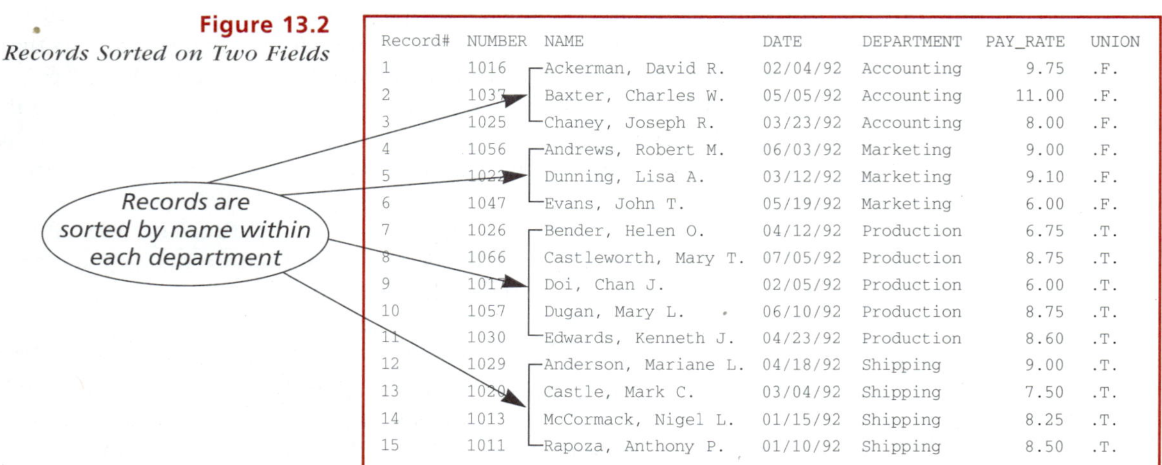
Records are
sorted by name within
each department

Record#	NUMBER	NAME	DATE	DEPARTMENT	PAY_RATE	UNION
1	1016	Ackerman, David R.	02/04/92	Accounting	9.75	.F.
2	1037	Baxter, Charles W.	05/05/92	Accounting	11.00	.F.
3	1025	Chaney, Joseph R.	03/23/92	Accounting	8.00	.F.
4	1056	Andrews, Robert M.	06/03/92	Marketing	9.00	.F.
5	1022	Dunning, Lisa A.	03/12/92	Marketing	9.10	.F.
6	1047	Evans, John T.	05/19/92	Marketing	6.00	.F.
7	1026	Bender, Helen O.	04/12/92	Production	6.75	.T.
8	1066	Castleworth, Mary T.	07/05/92	Production	8.75	.T.
9	1017	Doi, Chan J.	02/05/92	Production	6.00	.T.
10	1057	Dugan, Mary L.	06/10/92	Production	8.75	.T.
11	1030	Edwards, Kenneth J.	04/23/92	Production	8.60	.T.
12	1029	Anderson, Mariane L.	04/18/92	Shipping	9.00	.T.
13	1020	Castle, Mark C.	03/04/92	Shipping	7.50	.T.
14	1013	McCormack, Nigel L.	01/15/92	Shipping	8.25	.T.
15	1011	Rapoza, Anthony P.	01/10/92	Shipping	8.50	.T.

Figure 13.2
Records Sorted on Two Fields

Sorting on two (or more) keys is very similar to sorting on a single key. The only difference concerns the sort key. Instead of selecting one key, you must select two. Further, you *must* select the more important sort key (called the **major key**) first. Then you select the less important sort key (called the **minor key**). In the example, you would select DEPARTMENT and then NAME.

Removing Files (105)

Sometimes you want to remove a file from your catalog and delete it from your disk. If you never remove files, your disk and your catalogs can become cluttered quickly. Thus, if you have files that you don't think you will need again, it's a good idea to remove them. In your case, the sorted file is a good candidate for removal once you have used it to display the sorted data. After all, once you make any further changes in EMPLOYEE, the data in this file is out of date. If you need it again later, you can re-create it using the new data in EMPLOYEE.

TUTORIAL

In this tutorial, you sort a database file and then display the sorted data.

1 Sort the EMPLOYEE database file on the NAME field. Call the sorted file SORTFLE.

Select	EMPLOYEE	from Data column of Control Center.
Select	"Modify structure/order"	

Note that you make this selection rather than "Use file" as you usually do. You are then taken to the Database Design screen.

Select	"Sort database on field list"	from Organize menu.

Your screen should then look like Figure 13.3. dBASE is now prompting you to indicate the key field. You could simply type the name of the field you want, but it is usually simpler to press Shift-F1. This produces a *pick list*, which is simply a list of items from which you can choose.

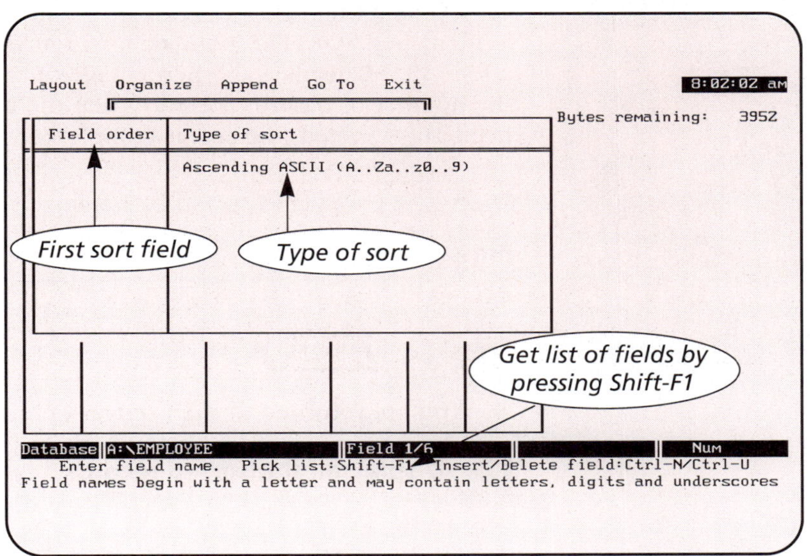

Figure 13.3
Database Design Screen

Press	SHIFT - F1	Produces list of available fields.
Select	"NAME"	
Press	↵ ENTER	Selects sort key.

You actually pressed Enter twice. The first time completed the selection of NAME. The second time indicated that the sort key was complete. Next you indicate the type of sort you want. The type of sort currently shown on the screen is called "Ascending ASCII." The entry in parentheses describes this sort. Other sort types are available in dBASE. To change from one to another, press the spacebar (just as you did to change from one field type to another when you first designed your database). The types you cycle through are Descending ASCII (z..aZ..A9..0), Ascending Dictionary (Aa..Zz0..9), and Descending Dictionary (zZ..aA9..0). Usually you select "Ascending ASCII," but it's nice to know the others are available. In this text, unless you are specifically told otherwise, select "Ascending ASCII." This sequence is already on the screen.

Press	↵ ENTER	Selects sort type.

You could now enter a second sort key if you wished. In this example, you have no second sort key.

Press	↵ ENTER	Indicates no additional sort keys.
Type	SORTFLE	
Press	↵ ENTER	Names sorted file.

If dBASE indicates the file exists and asks if it is all right to overwrite the existing file, press Y. (This only happens if you have previously created a file named SORTFLE.) The data will now be sorted. During the sort operation, dBASE displays the percentage of the file that has been sorted and the number of records sorted. When the message indicates that the file has been 100% sorted, the sort is completed.

Type	Employees sorted by name	
Press	↵ ENTER	Describes sorted file.
Select	"Save changes and exit"	from Exit menu.
Press	↵ ENTER	

You are returned to the Control Center.

2 Display all the sorted records.

Activate	SORTFLE

Remember that the "Sort" option simply creates the file; it does not activate it. If after completing a sort, you immediately display records, they will not be in the order you have specified. You may think the sort has not even worked or that you must have made a mistake. The only thing wrong is that you are working with the wrong file: your original database file rather than the sorted version. Be sure you activate the sorted version before you attempt to display your data.

Press	F2 once or twice	Moves to Browse screen.

Your screen should look like Figure 13.4. Notice that the records are indeed sorted by name.

Figure 13.4
Browse Screen

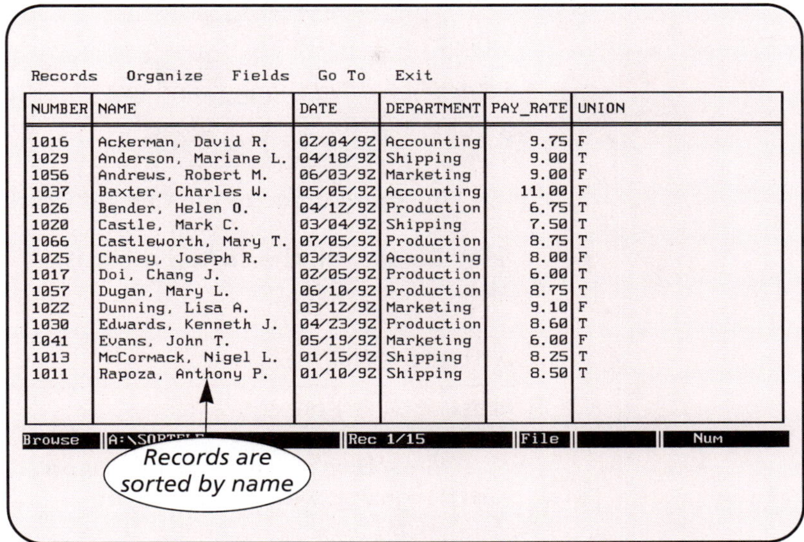

NUMBER	NAME	DATE	DEPARTMENT	PAY_RATE	UNION
1016	Ackerman, David R.	02/04/92	Accounting	9.75	F
1029	Anderson, Mariane L.	04/18/92	Shipping	9.00	T
1056	Andrews, Robert M.	06/03/92	Marketing	9.00	F
1037	Baxter, Charles W.	05/05/92	Accounting	11.00	F
1026	Bender, Helen O.	04/12/92	Production	6.75	T
1020	Castle, Mark C.	03/04/92	Shipping	7.50	T
1066	Castleworth, Mary T.	07/05/92	Production	8.75	T
1025	Chaney, Joseph R.	03/23/92	Accounting	8.00	F
1017	Doi, Chang J.	02/05/92	Production	6.00	T
1057	Dugan, Mary L.	06/10/92	Production	8.75	T
1022	Dunning, Lisa A.	03/12/92	Marketing	9.10	F
1030	Edwards, Kenneth J.	04/23/92	Production	8.60	T
1041	Evans, John T.	05/19/92	Marketing	6.00	F
1013	McCormack, Nigel L.	01/15/92	Shipping	8.25	T
1011	Rapoza, Anthony P.	01/10/92	Shipping	8.50	T

Select	"Exit"	from Exit menu.

You are returned to the Control Center.

3 **Sort the EMPLOYEE database file on the NAME field within the DEPARTMENT field.** Call the sorted file SORTFLE.

Select	EMPLOYEE	from Data column of Control Center.
Select	"Modify structure/order"	
Select	"Sort database on field list"	from Organize menu.
Press	SHIFT-F1	Produces list of available fields.
Select	DEPARTMENT	
Press	↵ ENTER	Selects first sort key.
Press	↵ ENTER	Selects sort type.
Press	SHIFT-F1	Produces list of available fields.
Select	NAME	
Press	↵ ENTER	Selects second sort key.

Press	↵ ENTER	Selects sort type.
Press	↵ ENTER	Indicates no additional sort keys.
Type	SORTFLE	
Press	↵ ENTER	Names sorted file.
Select	"Overwrite"	Overwrites existing file.
Select	"Save changes and exit"	from Exit menu.
Press	↵ ENTER	

You are returned to the Control Center.

4 Display all the sorted records.

Activate	SORTFLE	
Press	F2 once or twice	Moves to Browse screen.

Your screen should look like Figure 13.5. Notice that the records are sorted by name within department.

Select	"Exit"	from Exit menu.

You are returned to the Control Center.

Figure 13.5
Browse Screen

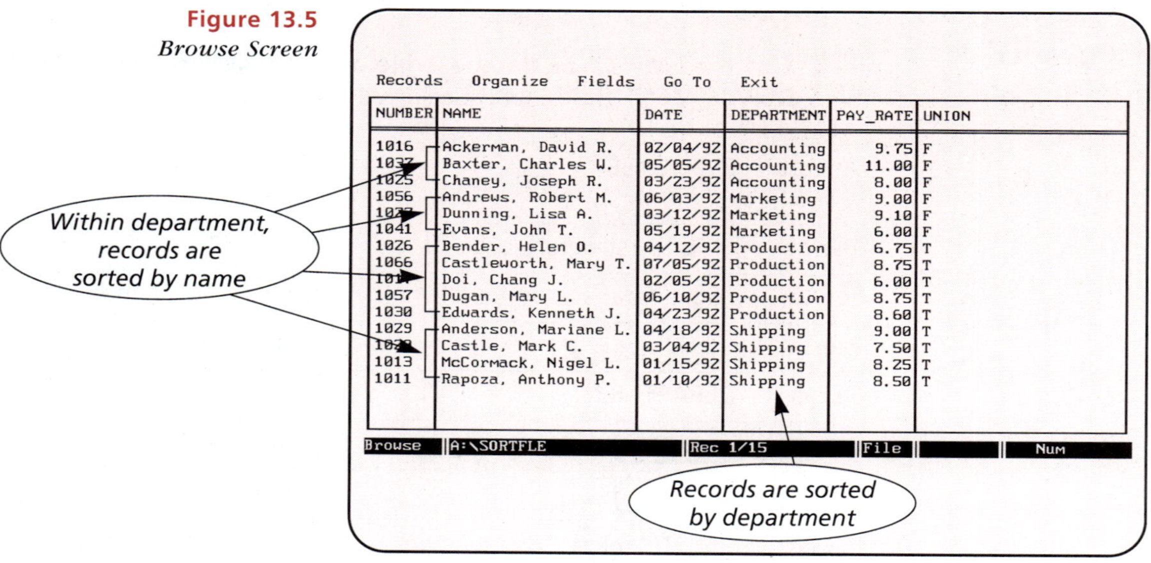

Records Organize Fields Go To Exit

NUMBER	NAME	DATE	DEPARTMENT	PAY_RATE	UNION
1016	Ackerman, David R.	02/04/92	Accounting	9.75	F
1037	Baxter, Charles W.	05/05/92	Accounting	11.00	F
1025	Chaney, Joseph R.	03/23/92	Accounting	8.00	F
1056	Andrews, Robert M.	06/03/92	Marketing	9.00	F
10[illegible]	Dunning, Lisa A.	03/12/92	Marketing	9.10	F
1041	Evans, John T.	05/19/92	Marketing	6.00	F
1026	Bender, Helen O.	04/12/92	Production	6.75	T
1066	Castleworth, Mary T.	07/05/92	Production	8.75	T
10[illegible]	Doi, Chang J.	02/05/92	Production	6.00	T
1057	Dugan, Mary L.	06/10/92	Production	8.75	T
1030	Edwards, Kenneth J.	04/23/92	Production	8.60	T
1029	Anderson, Mariane L.	04/18/92	Shipping	9.00	T
10[illegible]	Castle, Mark C.	03/04/92	Shipping	7.50	T
1013	McCormack, Nigel L.	01/15/92	Shipping	8.25	T
1011	Rapoza, Anthony P.	01/10/92	Shipping	8.50	T

Browse | A:\SORTFLE | Rec 1/15 | File | | Num

Within department, records are sorted by name
Records are sorted by department

5 Remove SORTFLE from your catalog and delete it from your disk.

Press	(arrow keys)	Moves highlight to SORTFLE.

To delete a file, it must *not* be active. If it is (that is, if it appears above the line), you must deactivate it.

Press	↵ ENTER	
Select	"Close file"	Deactivates file.

You can now remove the file from the catalog.

Press	(arrow keys)	Moves highlight to file.
Select	"Remove highlighted file from catalog"	from Catalog menu.

As a safety feature, dBASE asks you if you are sure you want to remove it from the catalog.

Select	"Yes"	Removes file from catalog.

dBASE asks you if you also want to remove it from the disk.

Select	"Yes"	Deletes file from disk.

PROCEDURE SUMMARY

SORTING A DATABASE FILE ON A SINGLE FIELD

Select database file to sort at the Control Center.	(your choice)
Select "Modify structure/order."	
Select "Sort database on field list" from the Organize menu.	
Produce pick list.	SHIFT - F1
Select sort key.	(your choice), ↵ ENTER
Select desired type of sort.	SPACEBAR
Complete selection.	↵ ENTER
Indicate there are no additional sort keys.	↵ ENTER
Type the name of the sorted file.	(your input), ↵ ENTER

If you are asked if it is all right to overwrite the existing file and you don't mind, select "Overwrite." If you don't want to overwrite the file, select "Cancel" and the sort will *not* take place.	(your choice)
Enter a description for sorted file.	(your input), ↵ ENTER
Select "Save changes and exit" from the Exit menu.	
Confirm that you want to exit.	↵ ENTER

USING A SORTED FILE

Activate the sorted file.	

SORTING ON MORE THAN ONE FIELD

Select database file to sort at the Control Center.	(your choice)
Select "Modify structure/order."	
Select "Sort database on field list" from the Organize menu.	
Produce pick list.	SHIFT - F1
Select first sort key.	(your choice), ↵ ENTER
Select desired type of sort.	SPACEBAR
Complete selection.	↵ ENTER
Produce pick list.	SHIFT - F1
Select second sort key.	(your choice), ↵ ENTER
Select desired type of sort.	SPACEBAR
Complete selection.	↵ ENTER
Indicate there are no additional sort keys.	↵ ENTER
Enter the name of the sorted file.	(your input), ↵ ENTER
If you are asked if it is all right to overwrite the existing file and you don't mind, select "Overwrite." If you don't want to overwrite the file, select "Cancel" and the sort will *not* take place.	(your choice)
Enter a description for sorted file.	(your input), ↵ ENTER

Select "Save changes and exit" from the Exit menu.	
Confirm that you want to exit.	↵ ENTER

REMOVING FILES

Move the highlight to file.	(arrow keys)
Select file.	↵ ENTER
Select "Close file."	
Select "Remove highlighted file from catalog" from the Catalog menu.	
Select "Yes" to remove it from the catalog.	
Select "Yes" to delete file from disk.	

EXERCISES

1. Sort the records in the CHECK database file by Check Number. Use SORTFLE as the filename for the sorted file.
2. After the records have been sorted, display the Check Number, Date, Payee, and Check Amount fields for all records.
3. Sort the records in the CHECK database file in alphabetical order by Payee within Expense type. Use SORTFLE as the filename for the sorted file.
4. After the records have been sorted, display the Expense Type, Payee, Amount, Date, and Check Number fields for all records.

Creating and Using Indexes

CONCEPTS You are already familiar with the concept of an index. The index in the back of a book contains important words or phrases together with a list of pages on which the given words or phrases can be found. An index for a database file is similar. Figure 14.1, for example, shows the EMPLOYEE database file along with an index built on employee names. (In technical terms, NAME is the **index key**.) In this case, the items of interest are employee names rather than key words or phrases. Each employee name occurs in the index along with the number of the record on which the employee name is found. If you were to use this index to find Helen Bender, for example, you would find her name in the index, look at the corresponding record number (8), and then go immediately to record 8 in the EMPLOYEE file, thus finding her much more

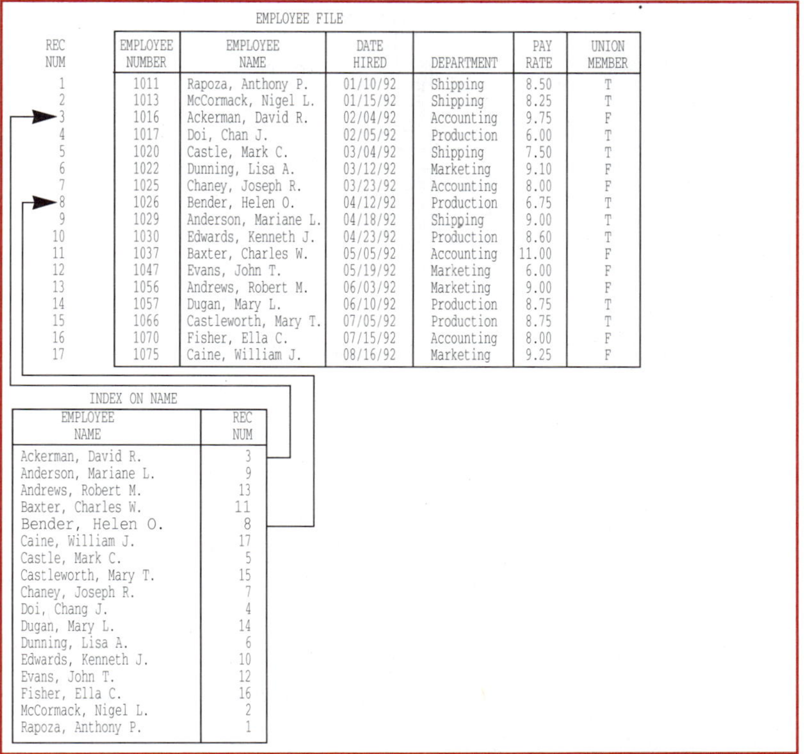

EMPLOYEE FILE

REC NUM	EMPLOYEE NUMBER	EMPLOYEE NAME	DATE HIRED	DEPARTMENT	PAY RATE	UNION MEMBER
1	1011	Rapoza, Anthony P.	01/10/92	Shipping	8.50	T
2	1013	McCormack, Nigel L.	01/15/92	Shipping	8.25	T
3	1016	Ackerman, David R.	02/04/92	Accounting	9.75	F
4	1017	Doi, Chan J.	02/05/92	Production	6.00	T
5	1020	Castle, Mark C.	03/04/92	Shipping	7.50	T
6	1022	Dunning, Lisa A.	03/12/92	Marketing	9.10	F
7	1025	Chaney, Joseph R.	03/23/92	Accounting	8.00	F
8	1026	Bender, Helen O.	04/12/92	Production	6.75	T
9	1029	Anderson, Mariane L.	04/18/92	Shipping	9.00	T
10	1030	Edwards, Kenneth J.	04/23/92	Production	8.60	T
11	1037	Baxter, Charles W.	05/05/92	Accounting	11.00	F
12	1047	Evans, John T.	05/19/92	Marketing	6.00	F
13	1056	Andrews, Robert M.	06/03/92	Marketing	9.00	F
14	1057	Dugan, Mary L.	06/10/92	Production	8.75	T
15	1066	Castleworth, Mary T.	07/05/92	Production	8.75	T
16	1070	Fisher, Ella C.	07/15/92	Accounting	8.00	F
17	1075	Caine, William J.	08/16/92	Marketing	9.25	F

INDEX ON NAME

EMPLOYEE NAME	REC NUM
Ackerman, David R.	3
Anderson, Mariane L.	9
Andrews, Robert M.	13
Baxter, Charles W.	11
Bender, Helen O.	8
Caine, William J.	17
Castle, Mark C.	5
Castleworth, Mary T.	15
Chaney, Joseph R.	7
Doi, Chang J.	4
Dugan, Mary L.	14
Dunning, Lisa A.	6
Edwards, Kenneth J.	10
Evans, John T.	12
Fisher, Ella C.	16
McCormack, Nigel L.	2
Rapoza, Anthony P.	1

Figure 14.1
Use of an Index

rapidly than if you had had to look at each employee one at a time. This is precisely what dBASE does when using an index. Thus indexes make the process of retrieving an employee much more efficient.

There is another benefit to indexes, however. Indexes provide an efficient alternative to sorting. Look at the record numbers in the index and suppose you used them to list all employees. That is, you simply followed down the record number column, listing the corresponding employees as you went. In this example, you would first list the employee on record 3 (David Ackerman), then the employee on record 9 (Mariane Anderson), then the employee on record 13 (Robert Andrews), and so on. You would be listing the employees in name order *without sorting the file*. Provided you have such an index in place, there is no need to take the time to create a separate sorted version of the EMPLOYEE file.

Creating an Index on a Single Field 114

To gain the benefits from an index, you must first create one. Usually an index is created on a single field (like NAME). In other words, the index key is usually a single field. When you create such an index, you must specify a name (also called a **tag**) for the index along with the field that will be the index key.

Figure 14.2
Database Design Screen

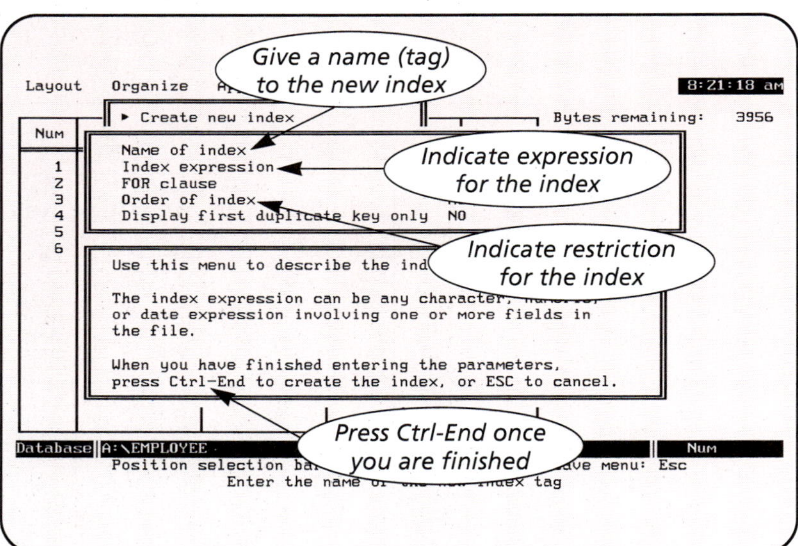

Creating an Index on More Than One Field 114

Although the index key is usually a single field, it can be a combination of fields. The steps in creating such an index are very similar to those used when the index is a single field. The only difference is that when you enter the index key, you must enter an expression that combines the fields.

Using an Index to Order Records 115

One use for indexes is as an efficient alternative to sorting. If you decide to use the index on the NAME field, for example, the records in the database file will *appear* to be in name order. If you instead use the index on the combination of the department and name field, the records will appear to be sorted by name within department. This allows you to have the records in the order you want without going through the process of sorting your database file.

Using an Index to Find a Record (115)

The other use for indexes is to allow you to rapidly find records. Using an index to locate a record is much more efficient than finding the record with the "Forward search" option. With the "Forward search" option, dBASE must examine each record in turn, until it finds the one you want. With an index, it can go directly to the desired record. To use an index in this way, you must activate it as the master index. Then you will be able to find records using the "Index key search" option of the Position menu.

Removing Unwanted Indexes (116)

Occasionally you might find that you created an index that you now never use. You should probably get rid of such an index because it occupies disk space. In addition, dBASE must keep this index up to date; that is, when you change the data in your database file, dBASE must make the appropriate changes to the index. If you are not going to use the index, there is no point in wasting the space or in having dBASE do the extra work.

TUTORIAL

In this tutorial, you create and use a variety of indexes for a database file.

1 Create an index on the NAME field of the EMPLOYEE database file.

Select	EMPLOYEE	from Data column of Control Center.
Select	"Modify structure/order"	
Select	"Create new index"	from Organize menu.

Note that some indexes already exist. Any field for which you entered the letter Y in the Index column already has an index. Thus you would not need to go through the process for these fields. When you select "Create new index," you see the screen shown in Figure 14.2. Use this screen to specify details about your index. To specify an index, you must give it a name, also called a **tag**. You must also specify the index key, that is, the expression on which the index is created.

Press	↵ ENTER

You are now ready to enter a name (tag) for the index.

> **TIP** If your index expression is a single field, it's a good idea to also use this field name as the index tag as has been done here.

Press	↵ ENTER	Prepare to assign a name to index. ◀
Type	NAME	
Press	↵ ENTER	Gives NAME as index tag.
Press	↵ ENTER	Enters index expression.
Press	SHIFT - F1	Produces pick list.
Select	NAME	
Press	↵ ENTER	Completes index expression.

You actually pressed Enter twice. The first time completed the selection of NAME. The second time indicated that the index expression was complete.

Press	CTRL - END	Indicates that you are done.

Notice that the entry in the index column for the NAME field has been changed to Y since this field now has an index.

Select	"Save changes and exit"	from Exit menu.
Press	↵ ENTER	

You are returned to the Control Center.

> **TIP** If your index expression is a combination of fields, it's a good idea to assign the index a tag that emphasizes the combination. In this case you are using DPTNAME (for DeParTment and NAME).

2 Create an index on the combination of the DEPARTMENT field and the NAME field in the EMPLOYEE database file.

Select	EMPLOYEE	from Data column of Control Center.
Select	"Modify structure/order"	
Select	"Create new index"	from Organize menu.
Press	↵ ENTER	

You are ready to enter a name (tag) for the index. ◀

Type	DPTNAME	
Press	↵ ENTER	Gives DPTNAME as index tag.
Press	↵ ENTER	Enters index expression.
Press	SHIFT - F1	Produces pick list.
Select	DEPARTMENT	
Press	+	

Press	SHIFT - F1	Produces pick list.
Select	NAME	
Press	↵ ENTER	Completes index expression.

This index expression indicates the combination of DEPARTMENT and NAME.

Press	CTRL - END	Indicates that you are done.
Select	"Save changes and exit"	from Exit menu.
Press	↵ ENTER	

You are returned to the Control Center.

Unfortunately, to build an index on a combination of fields, both fields must be of CHARACTER type. This means that you could not use the same technique to build an index on the combination of department and pay rate, for example. There are ways around this problem, but they are beyond the scope of this text. Fortunately the situations in which you would need to do this are not very common. If you ever find yourself in such a situation, consult the dBASE manual.

3 Use an index to list the employees alphabetically by NAME.

Activate	EMPLOYEE

Unless already active.

Press	F2 once or twice	Moves to Browse screen.

The Edit screen would have worked just as well. It is more common to use this feature on the Browse screen, however.

Select	"Order records by index"	from Organize menu.

The Organize menu is found on the Database Design screen, the Edit screen, and the Browse screen. You can use whichever is most convenient. Here it is most convenient to use it from the Browse screen because that is where you will view the records.

Select	NAME

This index is now used to order the records. Your display should look like Figure 14.3. Note that the records appear to be sorted by name.

Select	"Exit"	from Exit menu.

You are returned to the Control Center.

Figure 14.3
Browse Screen

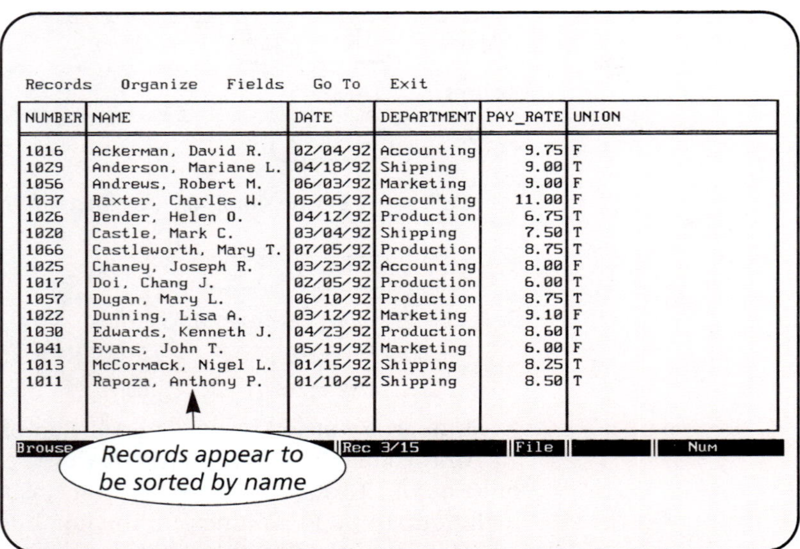

Records   Organize   Fields   Go To   Exit

NUMBER	NAME	DATE	DEPARTMENT	PAY_RATE	UNION
1016	Ackerman, David R.	02/04/92	Accounting	9.75	F
1029	Anderson, Mariane L.	04/18/92	Shipping	9.00	T
1056	Andrews, Robert M.	06/03/92	Marketing	9.00	F
1037	Baxter, Charles W.	05/05/92	Accounting	11.00	F
1026	Bender, Helen O.	04/12/92	Production	6.75	T
1020	Castle, Mark C.	03/04/92	Shipping	7.50	T
1066	Castleworth, Mary T.	07/05/92	Production	8.75	T
1025	Chaney, Joseph R.	03/23/92	Accounting	8.00	F
1017	Doi, Chang J.	02/05/92	Production	6.00	T
1057	Dugan, Mary L.	06/10/92	Production	8.75	T
1022	Dunning, Lisa A.	03/12/92	Marketing	9.10	F
1030	Edwards, Kenneth J.	04/23/92	Production	8.60	T
1041	Evans, John T.	05/19/92	Marketing	6.00	F
1013	McCormack, Nigel L.	01/15/92	Shipping	8.25	T
1011	Rapoza, Anthony P.	01/10/92	Shipping	8.50	T

Browse   Rec 3/15   File   Num

Records appear to
be sorted by name

4 Use an index to list the employees by NAME within DEPARTMENT.

Activate	EMPLOYEE	Unless already active.
Press	F2 once or twice	Moves to Browse screen.
Select	"Order records by index"	from Organize menu.
Select	DPTNAME	

This index is now used to order the records. Note that the records appear to be sorted by name within department.

Select	"Exit"	from Exit menu.

You are returned to the Control Center.

5 Use an index to locate employee 1037.

Activate	EMPLOYEE	Unless already active.
Press	F2 once or twice	Moves to Edit screen.

The Browse screen would have worked just as well. It is more common to use this feature on the Edit screen, however.

Select	"Order records by index"	from Organize menu.
Select	NUMBER	

This index is now used to order the records. It can also be used to rapidly retrieve records.

Select	"Index key search"	from Go To menu.
Type	1037	as search string.

If there were no such employee, dBASE would display a message indicating this. If, as is the case here, there is such an employee, this employee's record becomes the current active record (Figure 14.4).

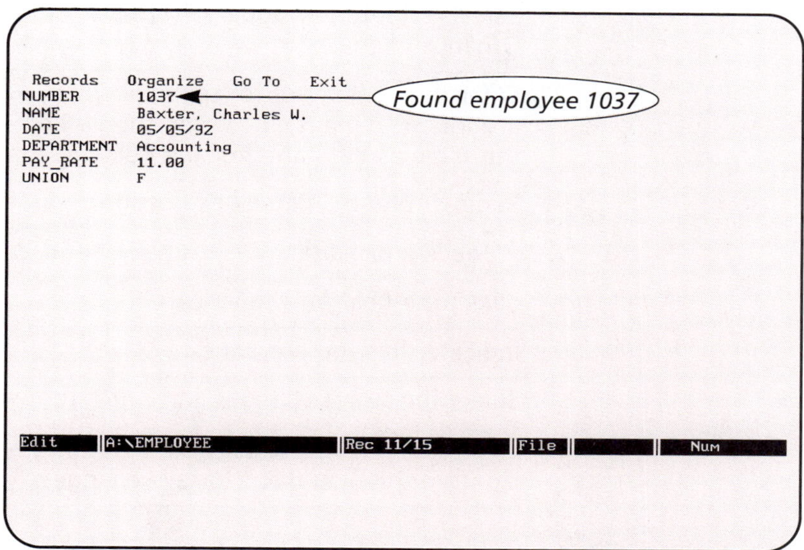

Figure 14.4
Edit Screen

Select	"Exit"	from Exit menu.

You are returned to the Control Center.

6 **Remove the index called DPTNAME.** It is no longer needed.

Activate	EMPLOYEE	Unless already active.
Press	F2 once or twice	Moves to Edit screen.
Select	"Remove unwanted index tag"	from Organize menu.

Select	DPTNAME	as index to remove.
Select	"Exit"	from Exit menu.

You are returned to the Control Center.

PROCEDURE SUMMARY

CREATING AN INDEX ON A SINGLE FIELD

Select the database file at the Control Center.	(your choice)
Select "Modify structure/order."	
Select "Create new index" from the Organize menu.	
Enter the name (tag) for the index. For a single field index, the name should be the same as the name for the field.	(your input), ↵ENTER
Begin entering an index expression.	↵ENTER
Produce a pick list.	SHIFT-F1
Select the field for the index.	(your choice), ↵ENTER
Indicate that you are done.	CTRL-END
Select the "Save changes and exit" from the Exit menu.	
Confirm that you want to save changes.	↵ENTER

CREATING AN INDEX ON MORE THAN ONE FIELD

Select the database file at the Control Center.	(your choice)
Select "Modify structure/order."	
Select "Create new index" from the Organize menu.	
Type the name (tag) for the index. The name should represent the combination of fields that you are using for the index.	(your input), ↵ENTER
Begin entering an index expression.	↵ENTER
Produce a pick list.	SHIFT-F1
Select the first field for the index.	(your choice)

Type a plus sign.	+
Produce a pick list.	SHIFT - F1
Select the second field for the index.	(your choice)
If the key has more fields, repeat the previous three steps for each additional field.	
Indicate the expression is complete.	↵ ENTER
Indicate that you are done.	CTRL - END
Select the "Save changes and exit" from the Exit menu.	
Confirm that you want to save changes.	↵ ENTER

USING AN INDEX TO ORDER RECORDS

Activate the database file unless it is already active.	(your choice)
Move to the Browse screen.	F2
Select the "Order records by index" option of the Organize menu.	
Select the tag for the index you want to use to order the records.	(your choice)
The records now appear to be ordered by this index.	

USING AN INDEX TO FIND A RECORD

Activate the database file unless it is already active.	(your choice)
Move to the Edit screen.	F2
Select the "Order records by index" option of the Organize menu.	
Select the tag for the index you want to use to find records.	(your choice)
Select the "Index key search" option of the Go To menu.	
Type the search string.	(your input)

If there is no matching record, dBASE displays a message indicating this. If there is such a record, it becomes the current active record and is displayed on the screen.

REMOVING UNWANTED INDEXES

Activate the database file unless it is already active.	(your choice)
Move to the Edit screen.	F2
Select the "Remove unwanted index tag" option of the Organize menu.	
Select the tag for the index you want to remove.	(your choice)

EXERCISES

1. Create an index called PAYEE on the PAYEE field in the CHECK database.
2. Create an index called EXPPAY on the combination of the EXPENSE and PAYEE fields in the CHECK database.
3. Use an appropriate index to list the records in CHECK in PAYEE order.
4. Use an appropriate index to list the records in CHECK ordered by EXPENSE within PAYEE.
5. Use an appropriate index to locate the record containing check 107.
6. Remove the index that was created on the combination of the EXPENSE and PAYEE fields.

Checkpoint 2

What You Should Know

- ✓ To position the record pointer to a record containing a certain value, use the "Forward search" or "Backward search" options of the Go To menu.
- ✓ To change records while viewing several records at a time, use the Browse screen.
- ✓ To make the same change to all records satisfying a certain condition, use an **update query**.
- ✓ Deleting records does not remove them from a database file. Rather, such records are marked for deletion. To physically remove such records from the file, use the "Erase marked records" option of the Organize menu on the Database Design screen.
- ✓ To mark records for deletion, use the Edit or the Browse screen. In either case, move to the record that is to be deleted and press CONTROL-U. The letters "Del" on the status line indicate that the current active record has been deleted.
- ✓ To unmark records that have been marked for deletion, use the Edit or the Browse screen. In either case, move to the deleted record and press CONTROL-U. The letters "Del" disappear from the screen.
- ✓ To mark all records that satisfy a certain condition for deletion, use an update query.
- ✓ To unmark all records that satisfy a certain condition, use an update query.
- ✓ To create a **custom form**, first activate the associated database file and then select <create> in the Forms column.
- ✓ To add blank lines to a form, press CONTROL-N.
- ✓ To select fields or text on a form, use F6.
- ✓ To move selected fields or text on a form, use F7.
- ✓ To place boxes on a form, use the "Box" option of the Layout menu.
- ✓ To use a custom form, highlight the form, press ENTER, and select "Display data."
- ✓ A **key field** is a field that is used as a basis of a **sorting** operation.
- ✓ To sort the records in a database file, producing a new database file, use the "Sort database on field list" option of the Organize menu.
- ✓ To sort on multiple keys, select the keys in order of importance.
- ✓ To display the records in a sorted file, the sorted file must be activated.
- ✓ An **index key** is the field or combination of fields on which an **index** is built. The name of an index is called a **tag**.

- ✓ To build an index, use the "Create new index" option of the Organize menu on the Database Design screen. Specify a name and expression for the index.
- ✓ To build an index on multiple fields, the fields should be CHARACTER fields. Enter the names of the fields, separated by plus signs.
- ✓ To make an individual index active, select it using the "Order records by index" option of the Organize menu on the Database Design screen. Records in the database file then appear to be sorted in order of the index key.
- ✓ An index may be used to allow rapid retrieval of individual records on the basis of the index key.

Review Questions

1. How do you use "Forward search" to find a record satisfying some condition?
2. How do you find the next record satisfying a condition?
3. How do you use the Browse screen to update records?
4. Which option allows you to use conditions to update records?
5. Which option allows you to use conditions to mark records for deletion?
6. How do you create an initial custom form? What does it look like?
7. How do you add blank lines to a custom form? Why might you want to do so?
8. How do you change the prompts on a custom form? Why might you want to do so?
9. How do you reposition prompts and fields on a custom form?
10. How do you add boxes to a custom form? What purpose do they serve?
11. How do you save a custom form?
12. How do you use a custom form? With which options do you use it?
13. How do you sort a database file on a single field?
14. How do you use a sorted file? At what point is a sorted file active?
15. How can you sort a database file on more than one field?
16. What is an index? What are the advantages associated with indexes? Describe the process of creating an index on a single field.
17. How can you create an index on more than one field?
18. How can you use an index to order records?
19. How can you use an index to find a record?

CHECKPOINT EXERCISES

The following exercises pertain to the MUSIC database file that you created in Checkpoint 1.

1. Use the "Forward search" option to find the music named Rio Rio.
2. Use the "Forward search" option to find the first record in the MUSIC database file that is of type CS.
3. Use the appropriate option to locate the next record of type CS.
4. Use the Browse screen to change the cost of Rio Rio to $9.95.
5. Use the Browse screen to change the price for Pardners to $6.95. In addition, change the type to LP and change the date to 2/24/92.
6. Use an update query to change the price of the music named Country Hills to $12.95.
7. Use an update query to add $1.00 to the amount of all records of type CD.
8. Use an update query to mark all records of type CD for deletion.
9. Use an update query to unmark all records of type CD.
10. Use the Edit screen to mark Passione for deletion.
11. Use the Browse screen to mark Moods for deletion.
12. Physically remove the marked records from the MUSIC database file.
13. List all the records in the MUSIC database file.
14. Create a form for the MUSIC database file that is similar to the form you created for the EMPLOYEE database file. Call it MUSFORM.
15. Activate this form. Select the Edit screen to make sure the form is active. (Select the "Exit" option of the Exit menu to leave the Edit screen option once you have seen your form on the screen.)
16. Sort the records stored in the MUSIC database file in alphabetical order by Artist Name. Use SORTFLE as the filename for the sorted file.
17. After the records have been sorted, print a list of all records using Quick Report.
18. Sort the records in the database file in alphabetical order by Music Name within Category. Use SORTFLE as the filename of the sorted file.
19. After the records have been sorted, print a list of all records using Quick Report.
20. Create an index on the Artist field in the MUSIC database. Use it to list the records in MUSIC in Artist order.
21. Create an index on the combination of the ARTIST and NAME fields in the MUSIC database. Use it to list the records in MUSIC ordered by NAME within ARTIST.
22. Use an index to locate the record on which the music name is Rio Rio.
23. Remove the index that was created on the combination of the ARTIST and NAME fields.

Creating a Report Design

CONCEPTS

In previous examples, you have looked at data using the Browse screen. You have also printed the data using Quick Report (Shift-F9). The format of the displayed output was very restrictive. Fortunately dBASE allows you to produce nicely formatted reports containing such items as a page number, date, page and column headings, and totals. Reports can thus be given a very professional appearance.

The report in Figure 15.1 lists the name, department, pay rate, and weekly pay amount for all employees. (The weekly pay amount is the pay rate multiplied by 40.) The top area of the report is called the **page header**. A page header appears at the top of each page in the report. The body of the report consists of **detail lines**. One of these is printed for each record. The bottom area, the one containing the total of the weekly pay amounts, is called the **report summary**. It appears once at the end of the report. Even if this report were 50 pages long, there would still be only one report summary and it would appear at the very end.

Figure 15.1
Weekly Payroll Report

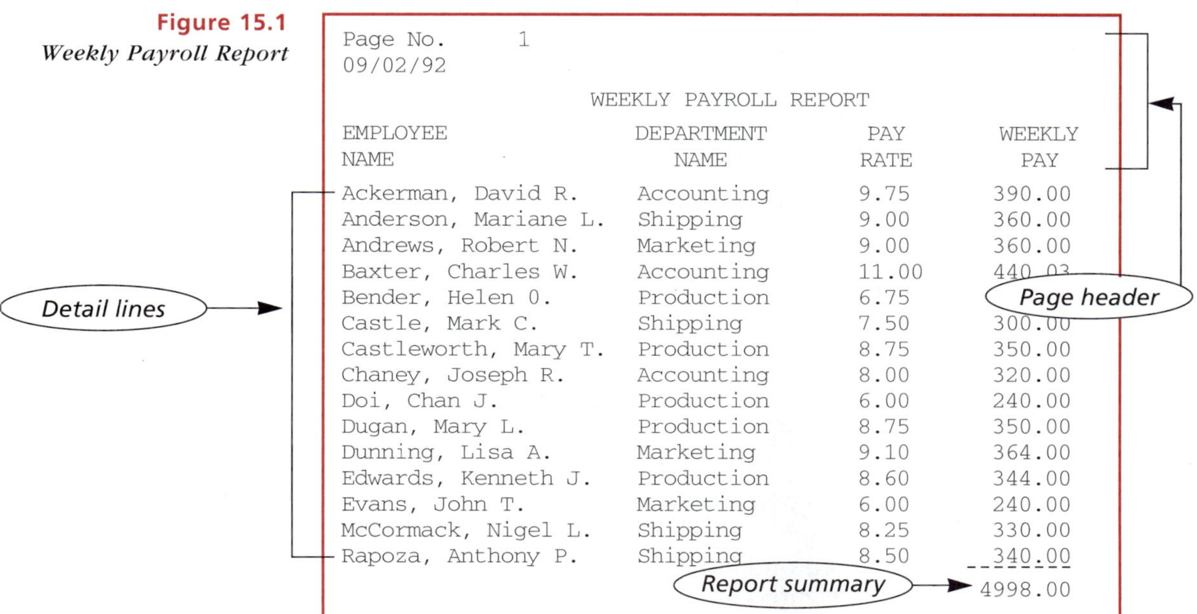

Page No. 1
09/02/92

WEEKLY PAYROLL REPORT

EMPLOYEE NAME	DEPARTMENT NAME	PAY RATE	WEEKLY PAY
Ackerman, David R.	Accounting	9.75	390.00
Anderson, Mariane L.	Shipping	9.00	360.00
Andrews, Robert N.	Marketing	9.00	360.00
Baxter, Charles W.	Accounting	11.00	440.0[illegible]
Bender, Helen O.	Production	6.75	[illegible]
Castle, Mark C.	Shipping	7.50	300.00
Castleworth, Mary T.	Production	8.75	350.00
Chaney, Joseph R.	Accounting	8.00	320.00
Doi, Chan J.	Production	6.00	240.00
Dugan, Mary L.	Production	8.75	350.00
Dunning, Lisa A.	Marketing	9.10	364.00
Edwards, Kenneth J.	Production	8.60	344.00
Evans, John T.	Marketing	6.00	240.00
McCormack, Nigel L.	Shipping	8.25	330.00
Rapoza, Anthony P.	Shipping	8.50	340.00
			4998.00

Figure 15.1 is quite typical of simple reports. The page header contains the date the report was produced, the title of the report, the page number, and headings for the various columns in the report. The detail lines contain values in various fields. The report summary contains a statistic, in this case, the sum of all the weekly pay amounts.

Sometimes you want to group records in a report; that is, you want to create separate collections of records sharing some common characteristic. In the report in Figure 15.2, for example, the records have been grouped by department. There are four separate groups: Accounting, Marketing, Production, and Shipping.

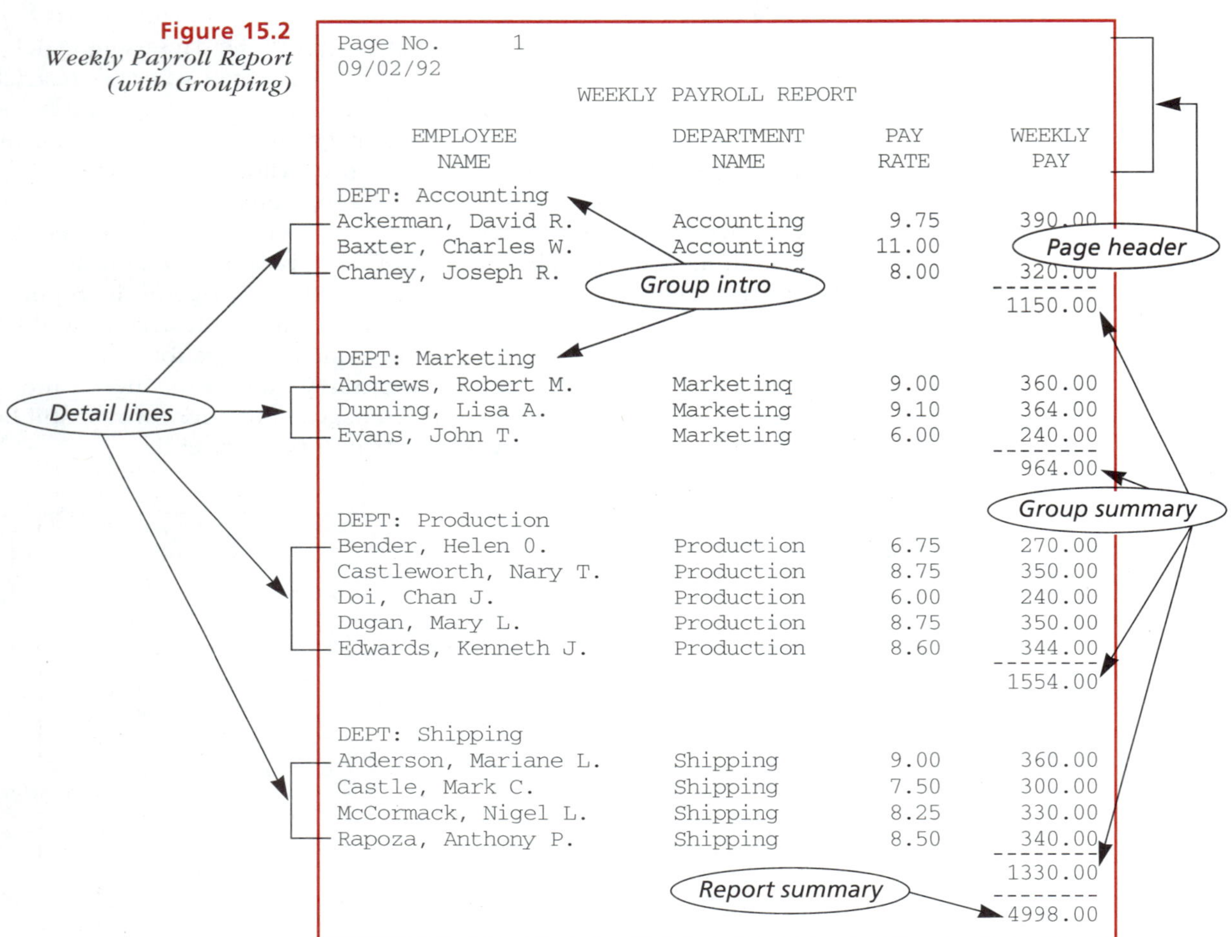

Page No. 1
09/02/92

WEEKLY PAYROLL REPORT

EMPLOYEE NAME	DEPARTMENT NAME	PAY RATE	WEEKLY PAY
DEPT: Accounting			
Ackerman, David R.	Accounting	9.75	390.00
Baxter, Charles W.	Accounting	11.00	
Chaney, Joseph R.		8.00	320.00
			1150.00
DEPT: Marketing			
Andrews, Robert M.	Marketing	9.00	360.00
Dunning, Lisa A.	Marketing	9.10	364.00
Evans, John T.	Marketing	6.00	240.00
			964.00
DEPT: Production			
Bender, Helen 0.	Production	6.75	270.00
Castleworth, Nary T.	Production	8.75	350.00
Doi, Chan J.	Production	6.00	240.00
Dugan, Mary L.	Production	8.75	350.00
Edwards, Kenneth J.	Production	8.60	344.00
			1554.00
DEPT: Shipping			
Anderson, Mariane L.	Shipping	9.00	360.00
Castle, Mark C.	Shipping	7.50	300.00
McCormack, Nigel L.	Shipping	8.25	330.00
Rapoza, Anthony P.	Shipping	8.50	340.00
			1330.00
			4998.00

Figure 15.2
Weekly Payroll Report (with Grouping)

When you group, you might include in your report two other types of objects: a group intro and a group summary. A **group intro** (or, formally, a group introduction) *intro*duces the records in a particular group. In Figure 15.2, the group intro indicates the department. A **group summary** provides some *summary* information about the records in the group. In Figure 15.2, the group summary gives the total of the weekly pay amounts for all records in the group.

Beginning the Report Creation Process

"Quick layouts" is a useful shortcut to starting a report. This option creates an initial report like the one shown in Figure 15.3. Before moving on, let's use this initial report to examine the screen's general characteristics.

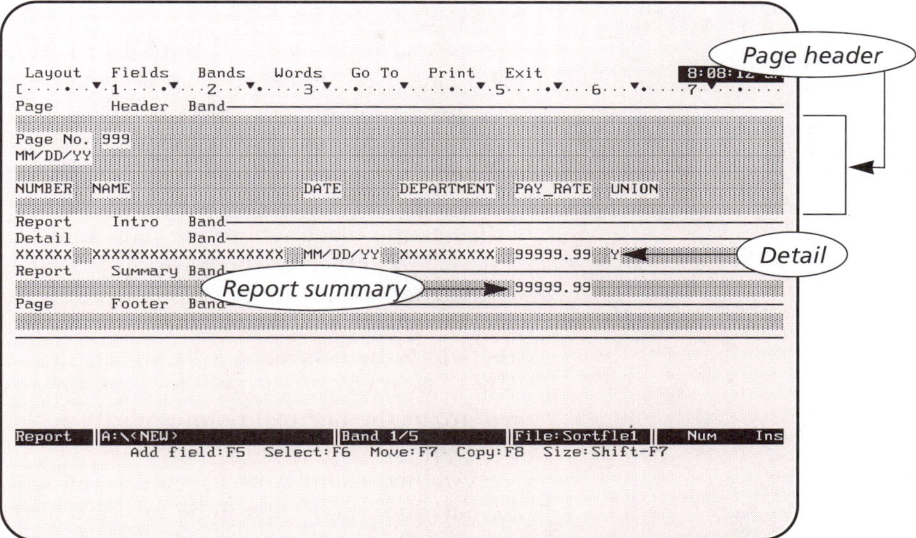

Figure 15.3
Report Design Screen

Each portion of the report is described in what is often termed a **band**. The page header band, detail band, and report summary band correspond to sections of the report you wish to create. There are also two other bands: a report intro band and a page footer band. A **report intro** appears once at the beginning of a report, regardless of how many pages the report contains. A **page footer** appears at the bottom of each page. Reports seldom require either a report intro or a page footer, although it's nice to have them available in case you run into a report that requires them.

To specify the layout of a report, you must describe each of the bands that you plan to include in the report. Thus you need to indicate the precise position of each item that will appear in the band.

At any given moment during the process, only one band is active. The active band is the band on which the cursor is currently positioned. To move from one band to another, use the UP and DOWN ARROWs. The band in which you are currently positioned is highlighted, indicating it is active. The number following the word "Band" on the status line contains the number of the active band.

Let's look at the specifics of the layout that dBASE has created for you (Figure 15.3). The block of lines that follows the words "Page Header Band" is the page header, and it prints at the top of each page. There is currently no report intro band. The detail band contains all the fields from the database file. The report summary band prints once at the end of the report.

In the page header band of the Report Design screen, you see such labels as Page No., NUMBER, NAME, DATE, and so on. These are printed on the page header exactly as they are shown here in precisely the same position. Thus Page No. prints on the second line of the page starting in the first column; NUMBER prints on the fifth line on the page starting in the first column; NAME follows NUMBER with two blank spaces in between; and so on.

Note also the 999 and MM/DD/YY. It certainly doesn't make sense to print Page No. 999 at the top of each page and then MM/DD/YY on the next line. Similarly you don't want each detail line to start with XXXXXX and then be followed by XXXXXXXXXXXXXXXXXXXX. Fortunately this is not what these symbols mean. They indicate the position at which the data in some particular field will be printed and what it will look like. The 999 indicates the place where the page number will appear on the report. The MM/DD/YY indicates the position in which the date will appear. The other 9s and the Xs indicate positions where various fields from your database file as well as additional calculated fields will appear. The 9s indicate that the field to be printed is a NUMERIC field, and the Xs indicate that the field is a CHARACTER field. In addition, if a NUMERIC field contains a decimal point, the decimal point appears at the correct position within the group of 9s.

You may wonder how you can tell whether the XXXXXX indicates that the data in some field will be inserted in the report at this spot or that the report will actually contain six Xs. Also, if XXXXXX is the data from some field, which field? Fortunately dBASE provides an easy way to tell. If you moved the cursor down to the group of Xs at the beginning of the detail band (Figure 15.4), you would see that the whole group becomes highlighted, not just the position where the cursor is. Notice also that a description of the NUMBER field appears on the last line of the screen. This indicates that the contents of the NUMBER field will be displayed at

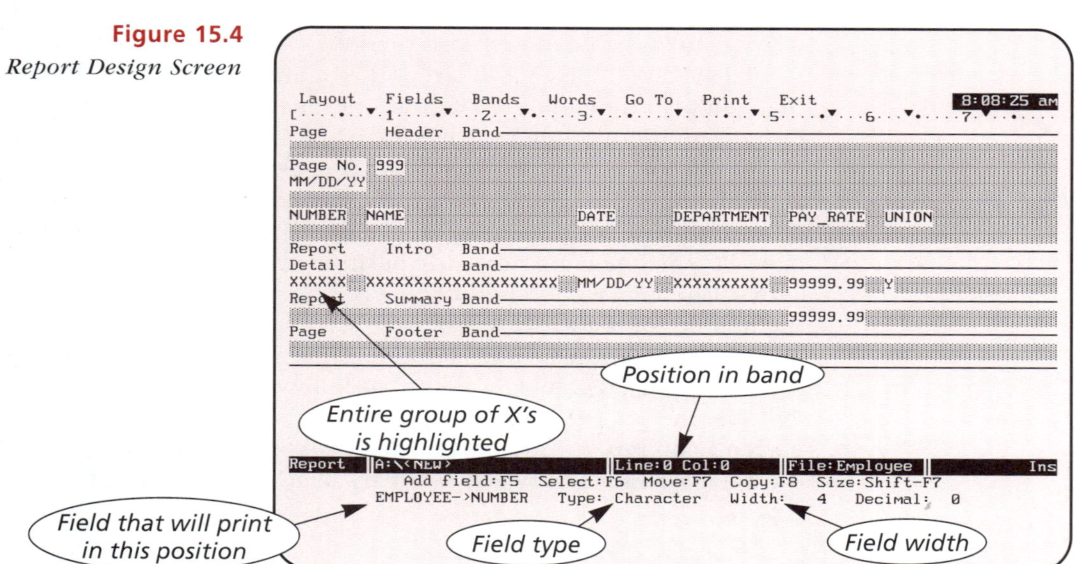

Figure 15.4
Report Design Screen

this position. Also notice that the line number and column number of the current cursor position in the band are both displayed on the status line. (Line numbers and column numbers both start with 0, rather than 1, as you might expect.)

Altering the Report Design 133

Once you have created the initial report design, you alter it, gradually transforming it into exactly the design you want. In the process, you will move fields, delete fields, resize fields, add new fields, and so on. You may also need to add lines to a band or delete lines from a band.

It is usually easiest to first transform the detail band. When the detail band is the way you want it, transform first the report summary band and then the page header band.

Adding or Deleting Lines in a Band 134

The process for adding or deleting lines in a band is very simple. It uses the following rules:

1. Press CONTROL-Y to delete the cursor line, the line on which the cursor is located.
2. Press CONTROL-N to insert a blank line before the cursor line.
3. Select the "Add line" option of the Words menu to insert a blank line after the cursor line.

These rules also furnish a convenient way to correct mistakes. The more you work with the Reports screen, the easier it will be to correct mistakes. But, until you become comfortable with the various correction methods, you can use the preceding three rules as follows:

- If you have an extra line you don't want, delete it with CONTROL-Y.
- If you need an additional line, insert one.
- If you have made mistakes on a particular line that you don't know how to fix, use CONTROL-Y to delete the line and then CONTROL-N to insert a new line. This combination erases the contents of the line. Now reconstruct the line the way it should be. ◀

TIP

Occasionally you might decide that it would be simpler to start over rather than make a number of individual corrections. If so, select "Abandon changes and exit" from the Exit menu. dBASE then asks you if you are sure you want to abandon the operation. Answer yes and you are returned to the Control Center without any of your work being saved. You can now start the process from scratch.

Selecting Fields and Text 134

dBASE allows you to easily move, delete, or resize fields on the screen. You can also move and delete text. By text, you mean simply characters. (On the current screen, the entries Page No., NUMBER, NAME, DATE, DEPARTMENT, PAY_RATE, and UNION are all text.) In any case, before you take any of these actions, you must *select* the portion of the screen with which you wish to work. You use F6 to select the field or text, and then you can take the appropriate action.

Removing Fields from a Report 134

To remove a field from a report, select it as you have done previously, and then press the DELETE key.

Moving Fields on a Report

135

To move a field, you must first select it. Then you can move the field by pressing F7, moving the cursor to the new location, and then pressing ENTER. As you move the cursor, you see a faint strip the exact size of the field move along with it. This helps you make sure you get the position you want. In some cases, getting the right position is not a problem. In other cases, though, this feature can be very handy.

In many cases, the field would be moved as soon as you pressed ENTER. In some situations, however, you need to take one additional step. If the new position causes a portion of the field to cover an existing field, you are asked: "Delete covered text and fields? (Y/N)." dBASE is warning you that the movement you are requesting would cause the deletion of an existing field. If this is acceptable, press Y and the move is complete. If not, press N and the move does not take place.

Resizing Fields on a Report

135

In some cases, you want to change the size of a field on a report. You may, for example, not need to allow as much space as dBASE has originally assigned to the field. If so, you can resize the field by selecting it, pressing SHIFT-F7, and then indicating the size you want.

Adding Fields

135

Sometimes you need additional fields. In the weekly pay report, for example, you need to add the weekly pay rate to the detail band. To add a field, move the cursor to wherever you want to place the field and then use the "Add field" option of the Fields menu.

Finishing the Report Design Process

136

Before saving the report, it's a good idea to view it on the screen. You can do this whenever you want by using the "View report on screen" option of the Print menu. If you discover anything you don't like about the report layout when you view it, you can change it at this time. Assuming the report is the way you want it, you can save it. The first time you save your report, assign it a name.

Modifying a Report Design

136

You can make changes to a report design whenever you want by highlighting the report at the Control Center, pressing ENTER, and then selecting "Modify layout." You are then returned to the Report Design screen with the current layout displayed. You can then make changes to the design using the same techniques you used when you first created it. Once you have finished, save your work and the changes are made permanent.

TUTORIAL In this tutorial, you create the weekly pay report.

1 Begin creating the weekly pay report. Call the report REPORT1.

Activate	EMPLOYEE	unless already active.
Select	<create>	in Reports column.
Select	"Quick layouts"	from Layout menu.
Select	"Column layout"	Creates an initial report layout.

> **TIP** You should use the "View report on screen" option often. In designing a report, you often move objects around on the screen. You add new fields, move existing fields, and delete existing fields. You change the text (letters) on the screen. It is helpful to see periodically just what the report will look like given the current entries on the screen. The "View report on screen" option gives you the opportunity to verify that you have done your work correctly.

Your screen should now look like Figure 15.3. Do not save your work at this point. Instead proceed directly to the next task.

2 View the current version of the report on the screen. When you have finished, save your work.

Select	"View report on screen"	from Print menu.

After a brief period, the report appears (Figure 15.5). As you can see, it looks just like the Quick Reports you produced earlier by pressing Shift-F9. Whenever you view a report on the screen, dBASE shows you the first screenful and then displays a message indicating that you should press Escape if you do not wish to see any more of the report or press the spacebar to see more.

Figure 15.5
Viewing Report

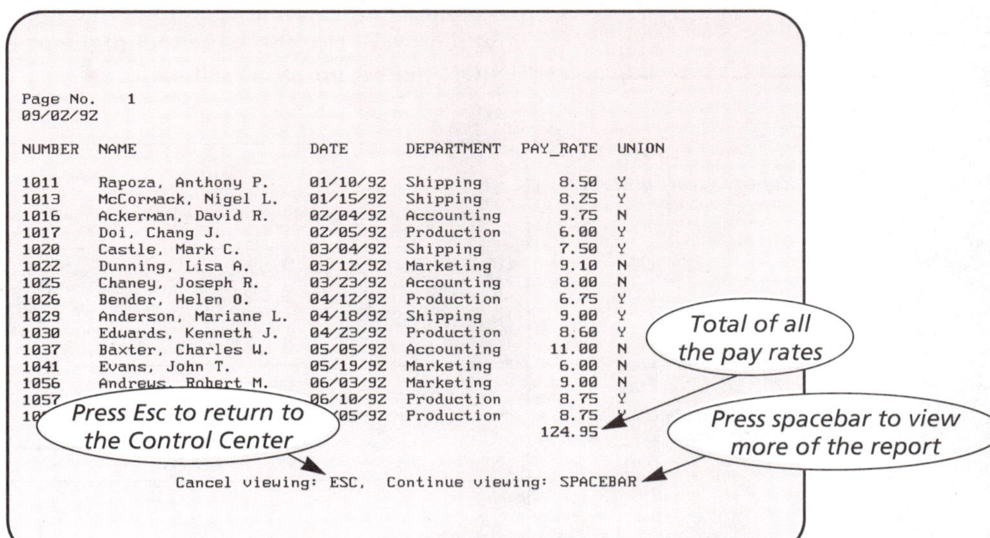

Page No. 1
09/02/92

NUMBER	NAME	DATE	DEPARTMENT	PAY_RATE	UNION
1011	Rapoza, Anthony P.	01/10/92	Shipping	8.50	Y
1013	McCormack, Nigel L.	01/15/92	Shipping	8.25	Y
1016	Ackerman, David R.	02/04/92	Accounting	9.75	N
1017	Doi, Chang J.	02/05/92	Production	6.00	Y
1020	Castle, Mark C.	03/04/92	Shipping	7.50	Y
1022	Dunning, Lisa A.	03/12/92	Marketing	9.10	N
1025	Chaney, Joseph R.	03/23/92	Accounting	8.00	N
1026	Bender, Helen O.	04/12/92	Production	6.75	Y
1029	Anderson, Mariane L.	04/18/92	Shipping	9.00	Y
1030	Edwards, Kenneth J.	04/23/92	Production	8.60	Y
1037	Baxter, Charles W.	05/05/92	Accounting	11.00	N
1041	Evans, John T.	05/19/92	Marketing	6.00	N
1056	Andrews, Robert M.	06/03/92	Marketing	9.00	N
1057	[illegible]	06/10/92	Production	8.75	Y
10[illegible]	[illegible]	[illegible]05/92	Production	8.75	[illegible]
				124.95	

Cancel viewing: ESC, Continue viewing: SPACEBAR

Press	(any key)	Returns to Report Design screen.
Select	"Save changes and exit"	from Exit menu.
Type	REPORT1	
Press	↵ ENTER	Names report file.

3 Correct the detail band on the weekly pay report.

Activate	EMPLOYEE	unless already active.
Select	"REPORT1"	in Reports column.
Select	"Modify layout"	Moves to Report Design screen.

The current design appears on the screen. You can now make changes to this design in exactly the same manner you did when you first created it. To move, delete, or resize a field, you first need to select the field.

TIP As you remove fields from the detail band, the page header will no longer be accurate. Don't worry about this. You will fix it shortly.

Press	↓ (as necessary)	Moves to NUMBER field in detail band.
Press	F6, ↵ ENTER	Selects field.
Press	DELETE	Deletes field.

Your screen should then look like Figure 15.6. Note that the field is now removed. Use the same technique to remove the DATE field and the UNION field from the detail band.

Figure 15.6
Report Design Screen

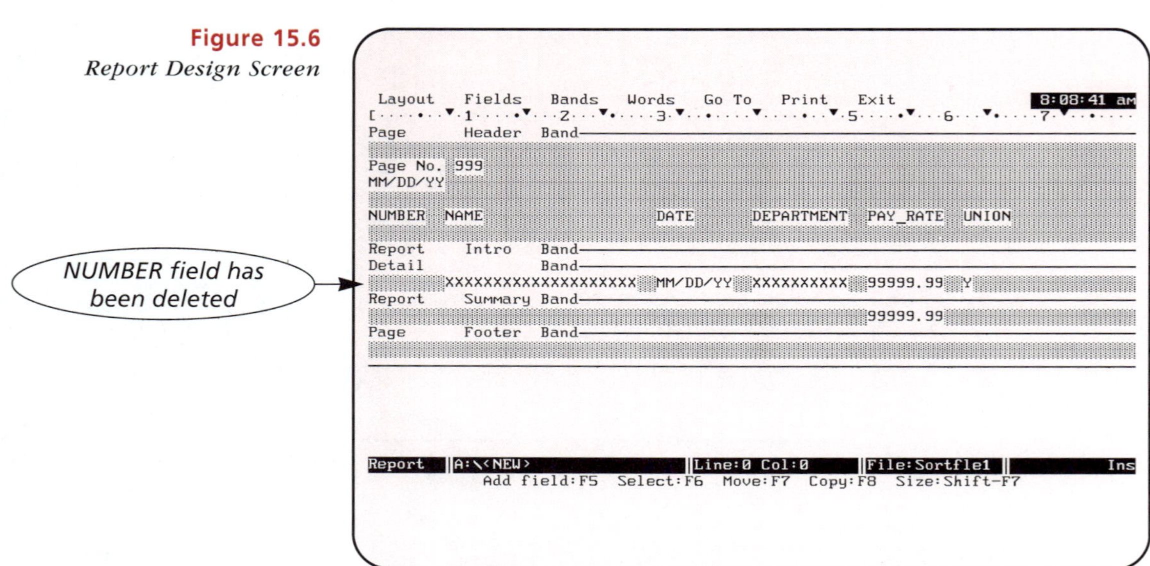

You now need to move the NAME field to the beginning of the band.

Press	← (as necessary)	Moves to NAME field in detail band.
Press	F6, ↵ ENTER	Selects field.
Press	F7	

Note the message near the bottom of your screen indicating that F7 is used to move a field.

Press	← (as necessary)	Moves to beginning of detail band.
Press	↵ ENTER	

dBASE warns you that the movement you are requesting would cause the deletion of an existing field. This is perfectly acceptable because you don't need the old NAME field.

Press	Y	Moves field.

Move the DEPARTMENT field in the same manner so that only one space separates it from NAME. Although you want to include the PAY_RATE field in the report, you don't need it to occupy as many positions as it currently does. Let's change it so that it only occupies five positions rather than eight (the decimal point counts as a position). The entry on the screen should read 99.99 rather than 99999.99.

Press	→ (as necessary)	Moves to PAY_RATE field in detail band.
Press	F6, ↵ ENTER	Selects field.
Press	SHIFT-F7, ← three times, ↵ ENTER	Changes size.

Now move the pay rate to the position shown in Figure 15.7. The only step that remains is to add the weekly pay rate to the detail band.

Figure 15.7

Report Design Screen

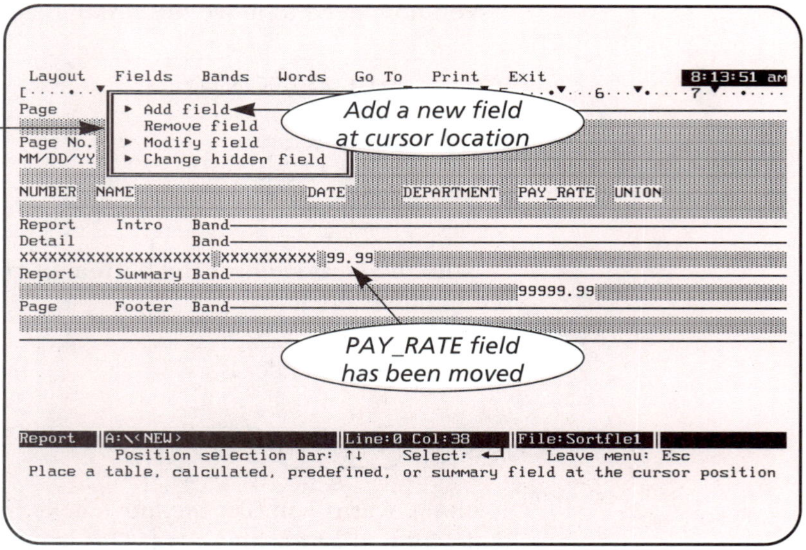

```
Layout   Fields   Bands   Words   Go To   Print   Exit                8:13:51 am
Page        ▸ Add field
            Remove field
Page No.    ▸ Modify field
MM/DD/YY    ▸ Change hidden field
NUMBER  NAME                      DATE        DEPARTMENT  PAY_RATE  UNION
Report    Intro    Band
Detail             Band
XXXXXXXXXXXXXXXXXXXX XXXXXXXXXX 99.99
Report    Summary  Band
                                                     99999.99
Page      Footer   Band
Report  A:\<NEW>                    Line:0 Col:38     File:Sortfle1
        Position selection bar: ↑↓    Select: ↵      Leave menu: Esc
 Place a table, calculated, predefined, or summary field at the cursor position
```

Fields menu

Add a new field at cursor location

PAY_RATE field has been moved

Press	→ (as necessary)	Moves cursor to follow PAY_RATE field with single space in between.
Select	"Add field"	from Fields menu.

The box on your screen shows the fields you can select to add to your report. The first column contains fields from your database file. The third column, PREDEFINED, contains special dBASE fields. The fourth column, SUMMARY, allows you to add fields that give statistics like sums and averages. These columns do not contain what you need, so you need to create an additional field that is calculated from existing fields (weekly pay is equal to PAY_RATE multiplied by 40).

Select	<create>	in second column (CALCULATED).
Press	↵ ENTER	
Type	WEEKLY_PAY	
Press	↵ ENTER	Names new field.
Press	↓ twice	Moves to "Expression."
Press	↵ ENTER	
Type	PAY_RATE * 40	
Press	↵ ENTER	Enters expression for new field.

This indicates that the value of WEEKLY_PAY for a record is to be obtained by taking the value of PAY_RATE on the record and multiplying it by 40. In these expressions, you can also use the plus sign (+) for addition, the minus sign (-) for subtraction, and a backslash (/) for division.

Press	CTRL-END	Adds field.

The new field has now been placed where you indicated. You now need to resize the field so that it is two positions smaller than its current size.

Press	← (as necessary)	Moves cursor into field.
Press	F6, ↵ENTER	Selects field.
Press	SHIFT-F7, ← twice, ↵ENTER	Changes size.
Select	"Save changes and exit"	from Exit menu.

4 Correct the report summary on the weekly pay report.

Activate	EMPLOYEE	unless already active.
Select	"REPORT1"	in Reports column.
Select	"Modify layout"	Moves to Report Design screen.

Next you need to move the cursor to the field representing the sum of pay rates in the Report Summary band (the group of 9s in the report band).

Press	↓, → (as necessary)	Moves cursor.
Press	F6, ↵ENTER	Selects field.
Press	DELETE	Deletes field.

Now you need to add the sum of the weekly pay amounts to the Report Summary band.

Press	← (as necessary)	Moves cursor.

Move your cursor so that it is directly below the first 9 in the group of 9s representing WEEKLY_PAY (the last group of 9s in the detail band).

Select	"Add field"	from Fields menu.
Select	"Sum"	from SUMMARY column.
Press	↓ three times	Moves to "Field to summarize on."

Press	↵ ENTER	
Select	WEEKLY_PAY	Selects field to summarize on.
Press	CTRL-END	Adds field.

The new field has been added, but it is the wrong size.

Press	← (as necessary)	Moves cursor into field.
Press	F6, ↵ ENTER	Selects field.
Press	SHIFT-F7, ← twice, ↵ ENTER	Changes size.

You need to make this field look more like a total by adding a line of hyphens right above the position where you have the sum of the weekly pay amounts.

Press	← (as necessary)	Moves cursor to beginning of line.
Press	CTRL-N	Inserts new line above cursor.
Press	→ (as necessary)	Moves cursor above first 9.
Type	--------	
Select	"Save changes and exit"	from Exit menu.

5 Correct the page header on the weekly pay report.

Activate	EMPLOYEE	unless already active.
Select	"REPORT1"	in Reports column.
Select	"Modify layout"	Moves to Report Design screen.

Now correct the page header so that it looks like the one in Figure 15.8.

Press	↓ four times	Moves cursor to line following MM/DD/YY.
Press	CTRL-Y twice	Deletes two lines.
Press	CTRL-N four times	Inserts four new lines.

Figure 15.8
Report Design Screen

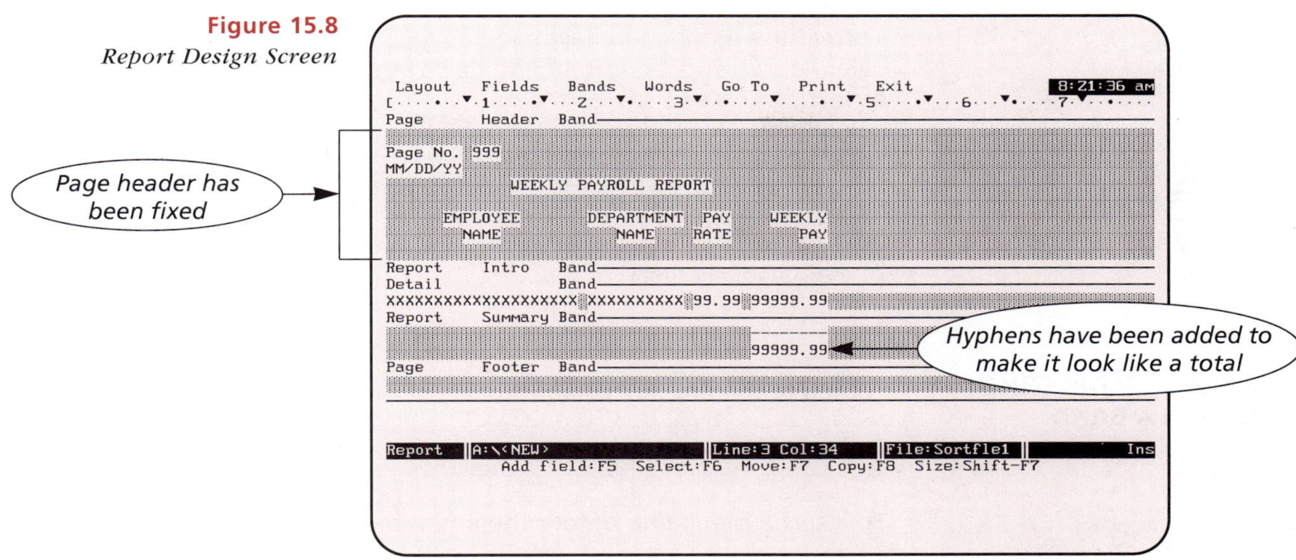

This erases everything underneath the page number and the date and gives you the right number of lines. To make any of the entries shown in the page header band in the figure, move the cursor to the desired location and type the letters you want. If you make a mistake, place the cursor on the incorrect letter and press the Delete key.

Select	"Save changes and exit"	from Exit menu.

PROCEDURE SUMMARY

BEGINNING THE REPORT CREATION PROCESS

Activate the database file.	(your choice)
Select <create> in the Reports column.	
Select "Quick layouts" from the Layout menu.	
Select "Column layout."	

ALTERING THE REPORT DESIGN

Correct the detail band by deleting, resizing, and/or adding fields or text. You may also need to add or delete lines.	(your input)

Correct the report summary band by deleting, resizing, and/or adding fields or text. You may also need to add or delete lines.	(your input)
Correct the page header band by deleting, resizing, and/or adding fields or text. You may also need to add or delete lines.	(your input)

ADDING OR DELETING LINES IN A BAND

To delete the line the cursor is on:

Delete the line.	CTRL-Y

To insert a blank line before the line the cursor is on:

Insert a line.	CTRL-N

To insert a blank line after the line the cursor is on:

Select "Add line" from the Words menu.

SELECTING FIELDS AND TEXT

To select a field:

Move the cursor to the field.	(arrow keys)
Select the field.	F6, ↵ ENTER

To select text:

Move the cursor to the beginning of the text.	(arrow keys)
Begin selecting the text.	F6
Move the cursor to the end of the text.	(arrow keys)
Complete selection.	↵ ENTER

REMOVING FIELDS FROM A REPORT

Select the field.	(your choice)
Delete the field.	DELETE

MOVING FIELDS ON A REPORT

Select the field.	(your choice)
Begin moving the field.	F7
Move the cursor to the new position for the field.	(arrow keys)
Complete the move.	↵ ENTER
If the new position would cover part of an existing field and this is acceptable, answer yes.	Y
If the new position would cover part of an existing field and this is not acceptable, answer no.	N

RESIZING FIELDS ON A REPORT

Select the field.	(your choice)
Begin resizing the field.	SHIFT - F7
Change the size of the field.	→ or ←
Complete the resizing.	↵ ENTER

ADDING FIELDS

To add an existing field:

Move the cursor to the position for the new field.	(arrow keys)
Select "Add field" from the Fields menu.	
Select the field.	(your choice)
Complete the process.	CTRL - END

To add a calculated field:

Move the cursor to the position for the new field.	(arrow keys)
Select "Add field" from the Fields menu.	
Select <create> in the CALCULATED column.	
Enter a name for the new field.	(your input), ↵ ENTER

Move to "Expression." (In these expressions, you can also use the plus sign (+) for addition, the minus sign (–) for subtraction, the asterisk (*) for multiplication, and the backslash (/) for division.)	↓
Select "Expression."	↵ ENTER
Enter the expression.	(your input), ↵ ENTER
Complete the process.	CTRL-END

To add a summary field:

Move the cursor to the position for the new field.	(arrow keys)
Select "Add field" from the Fields menu.	
Select the appropriate summary operator (such as "Sum") from the SUMMARY column.	(your choice)
Move to "Field to summarize on."	↓
Select "Field to summarize on."	↵ ENTER
Select the field.	(your choice)
Complete the process.	CTRL-END

FINISHING THE REPORT DESIGN PROCESS

Select "View report on screen" from the Print menu to verify that the design is correct.	
When you are satisfied with the design, select "Save changes and exit" from the Exit menu.	
If this is the first time you have saved this report, enter a name for the report file.	(your input)

MODIFYING A REPORT DESIGN

Activate the database file.	(your choice)
Select the report in the Reports column of the Control Center.	(your choice)
Select "Modify layout."	

EXERCISES

1. You are to create a report for data in the CHECK database file. The report is to contain page and column headings. Fields to be included on the report include the Check Number, Date, Payee, Check Amount, and Expense type. A final total is to be displayed of the check amount field. Begin the report creation process for this report. Call the report CHKRPT1.
2. Correct the detail band for this report.
3. Correct the report summary for this report.
4. Correct the page header for this report.

Printing a Report

CONCEPTS

A report file contains information about the layout (design) of a report. It contains details concerning the page heading, the layout of various columns, the totals that are to be calculated, and so on. The value of a report file is that, once it has been created, you can print a report using the design stored in the report file whenever you want. You do not have to specify the same details every time you print the report. You simply refer to the report file.

Printing a Report

141

At any point, you can print a report with the same layout as the one that was shown in Figure 15.1. You simply use the data in the EMPLOYEE database file together with the report file you have created. Certainly the data shown in the report will change. There could be new employees or changes in pay rates, for example. Nevertheless the "look" of the report remains the same. There will always be the same columns with the same column headings; the title will always be the same; the same columns will be totaled; and so on.

Sometimes you would like to have the records in a report ordered in some particular fashion. To do so, you just make sure the records in the database are ordered the way you want them to appear on the report. In this text, you do this by using an appropriate index. Another option would be to first sort the database file and then use the sorted file for the report.

Selecting Records for a Report

In many cases, you want to include all the records from your database file when you print the report. In other cases, you only want to include those records that satisfy some condition in the report. For example, the manager of the Accounting department may only be interested in employees who are in Accounting. Including other employees in the report would make it unnecessarily long. Further, the manager would need to skim through the report looking for just those employees in Accounting. It would be much simpler if the report could only include those employees. Fortunately you can easily restrict the records that appear in a report by using a query.

TUTORIAL

In this tutorial, you print the report you have created.

1 **Print the report whose description is stored in the report file called REPORT1.** Include all the records from the EMPLOYEE database file. The records should be ordered by name.

> **TIP** If the necessary index did not exist, you would create it using the techniques you learned in Topic 14.

Select	EMPLOYEE	from Data column of Control Center.
Select	"Modify structure/order"	
Select	"Order records by index"	from Organize menu.
Select	NAME	Orders records by name.

This technique assumes the appropriate index already exists. ◀

Select	"Save changes and exit"	from Exit menu.
Press	↵ ENTER	Confirms that you want to save.

You are returned to the Control Center. The records will be ordered by name.

Select	REPORT1	in Reports column.
Select	"Print report"	

You then see the same Print menu that you encountered on the Report screen. All the options function in exactly the same way. You could see the report on the screen by selecting "View report on screen." You could change the length of a page or the line spacing using the "Page dimensions" option. You now print the report.

> **TIP** If you happen to have already created and saved a query that contains the specific records you need, you can simply activate the query. To do so, highlight it in the Queries column, press Enter, and then select "Use view." You can then skip to the step where you select the report.

Select	"Begin printing"	
Press	(any key)	Prints report.

2 **Print the report whose description is stored in the report file called REPORT1.** Include only the employees in the Shipping department. You can restrict the records that will appear in a report by creating and using an appropriate query. Because you need the query only for this printing of the report, call it TEMP. This indicates that you consider the query to be temporary; that is, once you print the report, you no longer need the query. ◀

Activate	EMPLOYEE	unless already active.
Select	<create>	in Queries column.
Press	TAB four times	Moves to DEPARTMENT column.
Type	"Shipping"	
Press	↵ ENTER	Completes condition.
Select	"Save changes and exit"	from Exit menu.

Type	TEMP	
Press	↵ ENTER	Names query.

Because the query was just created, it is currently active. Thus you can use it to print the report.

Select	REPORT1	in Reports column.
Select	"Print report"	

The report was created for the EMPLOYEE database file. The question on the screen asks you if it is acceptable to use the view that is currently active rather than the EMPLOYEE database file for printing the report. You want dBASE to use the view.

Select	"Current view"	Allows dBASE to use active view for report.
Select	"Begin printing"	
Press	(any key)	Prints report.

Because you do not anticipate needing the TEMP query again, you should delete it from the catalog and from the disk. To do so, you must first deactivate it.

Select	TEMP	in Queries column.
Select	"Close view"	Deactivates query.

Now you can delete it.

Press	↓ (as necessary)	Highlights TEMP.
Select	"Remove highlighted file from catalog"	from Catalog menu.
Select	"Yes"	Removes file from catalog.
Select	"Yes"	Removes file from disk.

PROCEDURE SUMMARY

PRINTING A REPORT

Activate the database file. If an index is required to order the records a particular way, order the records by the index.	(your choice)
Select the report in the Reports column.	(your choice)

Select "Print report."	
Select "Begin printing."	

SELECTING RECORDS FOR A REPORT

Activate the database file.	
Select <create> in the Queries column.	
Enter the condition that identifies the records that should appear in the report.	(your input)
Select "Save changes and exit" from the Exit menu.	
Enter a name for the query. If you only need the query for this particular printing of the report, give it a name that emphasizes its temporary nature (for example, TEMP).	(your input), ↵ENTER
Select the report in the Reports column.	(your choice)
Select "Print report."	
Select "Current view."	
Select "Begin printing."	
Select the query you are using in the Queries column.	
Select "Close file" to deactivate query.	
Select "Remove highlighted file from catalog."	
Select "Yes" to remove it from the catalog.	
Select "Yes" to remove it from disk.	

EXERCISES

1. Print a report of all the records in the CHECK database file. Use the report layout stored in CHKRPT1.
2. Print a report of those records in the CHECK database file on which amount is more than $50.00. Use the report layout stored in CHKRPT1.

TOPIC 17

Including Subtotals

CONCEPTS

Often you need to group together in a report all the records that have the same value in some field. For example, you might want all the employees in any given department to appear together on the report. When you group records in this fashion, you may be interested in the totals for the records in each group. After the list of employees in a department, for example, you may want to see the total of the pay rates for just those employees. Such totals are called *subtotals* because they represent a subset of the overall total. The report shown in Figure 15.2, for example, contains subtotals of the weekly pay amounts for the employees in each department.

Grouping

148

The report in Figure 15.2 included two new types of objects: a group intro and a group summary. The group intro indicates the department and the group summary gives the total of the weekly pay amounts for all records in the group. To group records in a report, you need to use a new type of band, called a **group band**.

When you have added group bands to your report, your screen should look like the one in Figure 17.1. Note that two new bands have appeared, one labeled "Group 1 Intro Band" and the other labeled "Group 1 Summary Band." The collection of all employees in the same department is a group. Whatever you specify in the Group 1 intro band is displayed immediately *before* each group (it *intro*duces the group). Whatever you specify in the Group 1 summary band is displayed immediately *after* each group (in other words, it provides a *summary* for the group).

Look at the report intro band and the Group 1 intro band in Figure 17.1. Do you notice a difference? A blank line follows the Group 1 intro band, but none follows the report intro band. Any band that does not have at least one line following it is *closed*, and the contents of the band, whatever they may be, will not be printed on the report. The other bands are *open*, and their contents will print. Currently the Group 1 intro band consists of just a single blank line. This will still appear on the report, however. The group of employees in any given department is preceded by a single blank line. To close a band that is currently open or to open a band that is currently closed, move the cursor to the line that gives the name of the band and press ENTER.

Figure 17.1
Report Design Screen

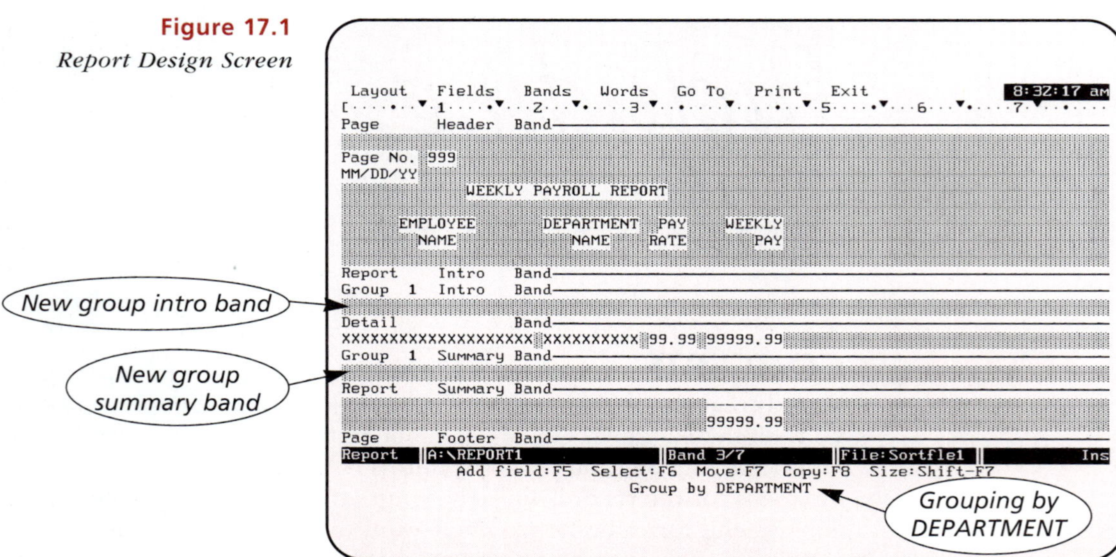

Printing a Report with Subtotals 148

The only special consideration in printing a report with subtotals is that the data *must* be in the correct order. Figure 17.2 illustrates what can happen if the order is not correct. This report is certainly very strange. There is a group for Accounting, followed by a group for Shipping, one for Marketing, and then *another* one for Accounting. What's wrong? The problem is that the records are not sorted correctly. All the records for a given department must be together for the report to be correct.

Figure 17.2
Weekly Payroll Report (with Incorrect Grouping)

WEEKLY PAYROLL REPORT

EMPLOYEE NAME	DEPARTMENT NAME	PAY RATE	WEEKLY PAY
DEPT: Accounting			
Ackerman, David R.	Accounting	9.75	390.00
			390.00
DEPT: Shipping			
Anderson, Mariane L.	Shipping	9.00	360.00
			360.00
DEPT: Marketing			
Andrews, Robert M.	Marketing	9.00	360.00
			360.00
DEPT: Accounting			
Baxter, Charles W.	Accounting	11.00	440.00
			440.00
DEPT: Production			
Bender, Helen O.	Production	6.75	270.00
			270.00

It is your responsibility to make sure that the data used for the report is sorted correctly. You can do so by sorting your database file appropriately and then using the sorted file for the report. Alternatively, you can use an index that orders the records appropriately.

TUTORIAL

In this tutorial, you change the report to include subtotals.

1 Modify the report stored in REPORT1 so that a subtotal is taken whenever there is a change in DEPARTMENT.

Activate	EMPLOYEE	unless already active.
Select	"REPORT1"	in Reports column.
Select	"Modify layout"	Moves to Report Design screen.

To group records in a report, you need to use a new type of band, called a group band. Add the necessary group band to the report.

Press	(arrow keys)	Moves to report intro band.

The group band follows the report intro band.

Select	"Add a group band"	from Bands menu.

At this point, you are asked to enter the value on which grouping takes place (Figure 17.3). You can enter a field value, an expression value, or a record count. You virtually always use a field value.

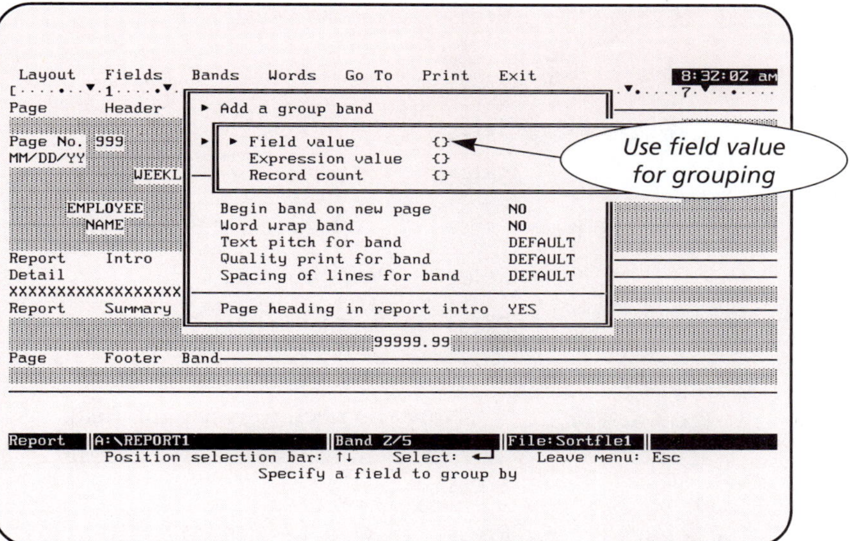

Figure 17.3
Report Design Screen

Select	"Field value"	
Select	DEPARTMENT	Selects field for grouping.
Press	(arrow keys)	Moves to beginning of first line of group intro band.
Type	DEPT:	
Press	SPACEBAR	
Select	"Add field"	from Fields menu.

You are then presented with a list of fields as you have seen before.

Select	DEPARTMENT	
Press	CTRL-END	Completes group intro band.

Now let's fix the group summary band.

Press	(arrow keys)	Moves to blank line in group summary band.
Press	CTRL-N twice	Adds two lines.
Press	(arrow keys)	Moves under first 9 in group of 9s for WEEKLY_PAY.

You should be on the first of the three blank lines in the group summary band.

Type	--------	
Press	(arrow keys)	Moves down one line and immediately under first hyphen.
Select	"Add field"	from Fields menu.
Select	"Sum"	
Press	↓ three times, ↵ENTER	Selects "Field to summarize on."
Select	WEEKLY_PAY	Selects field to summarize on.
Press	CTRL-END	Adds sum of WEEKLY_PAY to group summary band.

Now you need to resize the field.

Press	←	Moves cursor into field.
Press	F6, ↵ENTER	Selects field.

Press	SHIFT-F7, ← twice, ↵ ENTER	Resizes field.
Select	"Save changes and exit"	from Exit menu.

2 **Print the report.** You want the records to be ordered by name within department. You did have an index that you created on this combination, but you removed it. Thus you will need to re-create it. (If the index already existed, you would simply order records by this index.)

Select	EMPLOYEE	from Data column of Control Center.
Select	"Modify structure/order"	
Select	"Create new index"	from Organize menu.
Press	↵ ENTER	Enters name (tag) for index.
Type	DPTNAME	
Press	↵ ENTER	Gives DPTNAME as index tag. Moves to "Index expression."
Press	↵ ENTER	Enters index expression.
Type	DEPARTMENT+NAME	
Press	↵ ENTER	Completes index expression.
Press	CTRL-END	Indicates you are done.
Select	"Save changes and exit"	from Exit menu.
Press	↵ ENTER	

You are returned to the Control Center. Since you have just created the index ordering records by name within department, it is active. If not, you would first need to select the "Order records by index" option and then select the index.

TIP In actual practice, if you planned to print this report often, you would probably choose to retain this index.

Select	REPORT1	in Reports column.
Select	"Print report"	
Select	"Begin printing"	
Press	(any key)	Prints report.

Since this index was needed only for this report, you can remove it. ◀

Select	EMPLOYEE	in Data column.
Select	"Modify structure/order"	

Select	"Remove unwanted index tag"	from Organize menu.
Select	DPTNAME	Removes index.
Select	"Save changes and exit"	from Exit menu.
Press	↵ ENTER	Returns to Control Center.

PROCEDURE SUMMARY

GROUPING

Activate the database file unless it is already active.	(your choice)
Select the report in the Reports column.	(your choice)
Select "Modify layout."	
Move the cursor to the report intro band.	↓
Select "Add a group band" from the Bands menu.	
Select "Field value."	
Select the field on which to group.	(your choice)
Correct the group intro band using the same techniques you used to correct other bands.	(your input)
Correct the group summary band using the same techniques you used to correct other bands.	(your input)
Select "Save changes and exit" from the Exit menu.	

PRINTING A REPORT WITH SUBTOTALS

Activate the database file. If the data in the database file is not in the correct order for the report, select an index that will order the records appropriately. If no such index exists, create one.	(your choice)
Select the report in the Reports column.	(your choice)
Select "Print report."	
Select "Begin printing."	

EXERCISES

1. Modify the report format stored in CHKRPT1 so that a subtotal is taken when there is a change in Expense type.
2. Use this report format to display all the records in the CHECK database file. Be sure the records are ordered correctly.

Modifying the Structure

CONCEPTS When you initially create a database, you define its *structure*; that is, you indicate the names, types, and widths of all the fields. It would be nice if the structure you first defined would continue to be appropriate as long as you use the database. There are, however, a variety of reasons why the structure of a database file might need to change. Changes in the needs of users of the database might require additional fields to be added. For example, if it is important to store the number of hours an employee has worked, such a field must be added to the EMPLOYEE file since it is not there already.

Characteristics of a given field might need to change. It just so happens that Mary Castleworth's name is stored incorrectly in the database. Rather than "Castleworth, Mary T.", it should be "Castleworth, Marianne K.". There is no problem changing the middle initial from "T" to "K"; there is a big problem changing the first name from "Mary" to "Marianne," however. There is not enough room in the NAME field to hold the correct name! To accommodate this change, the width of the NAME field must be increased.

It may turn out that a field that is currently in the database file is no longer necessary. If no one ever uses the DEPARTMENT field, for example, there is no point in having it in the database file. Since the field occupies space and serves no useful purpose, it would be nice to remove it from the database file.

Sometimes you discover that the structure you determined earlier has some inherent problems. Did it ever bother you, for example, that you had to type a complete department name when entering each employee? Wouldn't it be easier to simply type a code number. This would make the process of entering data simpler. It would also save space in the database since storing a one- or two-character code number does not take as much space as storing a ten-character department name. Finally, it cuts down on errors during data entry. If you only have to type the number "01" rather than the name "Accounting," for example, you will be much less likely to make mistakes. Such mistakes can have serious consequences. If, for example, "Accouning" is inadvertently entered as the department for an employee, that employee will be *omitted* from any list of employees whose department is "Accounting." Thus you might want to store the code number rather than the department number. What do you do, however, if you are supposed to print the department *name* on some crucial reports?

The answer is that you create a separate database file containing department numbers and names. This would mean that rather than the single database file that you have been using (Figure 18.1), there will be two

Figure 18.1
Employee Data Stored in a Single File

EMPLOYEE NUMBER	EMPLOYEE NAME	DATE HIRED	DEPARTMENT NAME	PAY RATE	UNION MEMBER
1011	Rapoza, Anthony P.	01/10/92	Shipping	8.50	T
1013	McCormack, Nigel L.	01/15/92	Shipping	8.25	T
1016	Ackerman, David R.	02/04/92	Accounting	9.75	F
1017	Doi, Chang J.	02/05/92	Production	6.00	T
1020	Castle, Mark C.	03/04/92	Shipping	7.50	T
1022	Dunning, Lisa A.	03/12/92	Marketing	9.10	[illegible]
1025	Chaney, Joseph R.	03/23/92	Accounting	[illegible]	[illegible]
1026	Bender, Helen O.	04/12/92	Production	6.75	T
1029	Anderson, Mariane L.	04/18/92	Shipping	9.00	T
1030	Edwards, Kenneth J.	04/23/92	Production	8.60	T
1037	Baxter, Charles W.	05/05/92	Accounting	11.00	F
1041	Evans, John T.	05/19/92	Marketing	6.00	F
1056	Andrews, Robert M.	06/03/92	Marketing	9.00	F
1057	Dugan, Mary L.	06/10/92	Production	8.75	T
1066	Castleworth, Mary T.	07/05/92	Production	8.75	T

Department name

(Figure 18.2). Notice that the first database file has no DEPARTMENT column but instead has a column for code numbers (DEPT_NUMB). The second database file also has a DEPT_NUMB column as well as a column that contains the department name. Using these two database files still allows you to list the name of the department for each employee. To find the department name for Anthony Rapoza, for example, you would first find that he works in department 04 by looking in the DEPT_NUMB column in his row. Then you would look for the row in the second database file that contained 04 in the DEPT_NUMB column. Once you found it, you would look in the next column on the same row and see that department 04 is Shipping. Thus Anthony Rapoza works in the Shipping department.

You now have a database that consists of more than one database file. You need a way to relate the two database files, that is, to use information from both. This is done by using what is called a **view**. (You will create and use views in Topics 20 and 21.)

TIP When you change the width of a field, you should examine the reports and screens on which the field appears to see if they also need to be changed.

Changing Field Characteristics (158)

The original characteristics of a field (type and width) may no longer be appropriate. Typically, if you need to make a change, it is a width change such as increasing the width of the NAME field. Although not common, it is possible to change the type if necessary. ◀

TIP When you add a field, it does not automatically appear on reports or screens that you have already created. You must modify the reports or screens if you wish to include the new field.

Adding a New Field (158)

When a new field, such as the number of hours worked, becomes necessary, you must be able to add the field to your database file. ◀

To make new entries, you can use either Edit or Browse and simply proceed through each and every record. Whenever you encounter a record on which the value for DEPARTMENT is Accounting, set DEPT_NUMB to 01; if the value is Marketing, set DEPT_NUMB to 02; and so on. Does this approach seem cumbersome to you? Even with only seventeen records, it probably seems like a lot of busy work. What if there were several

Figure 18.2
Employee Data Stored in Two Files

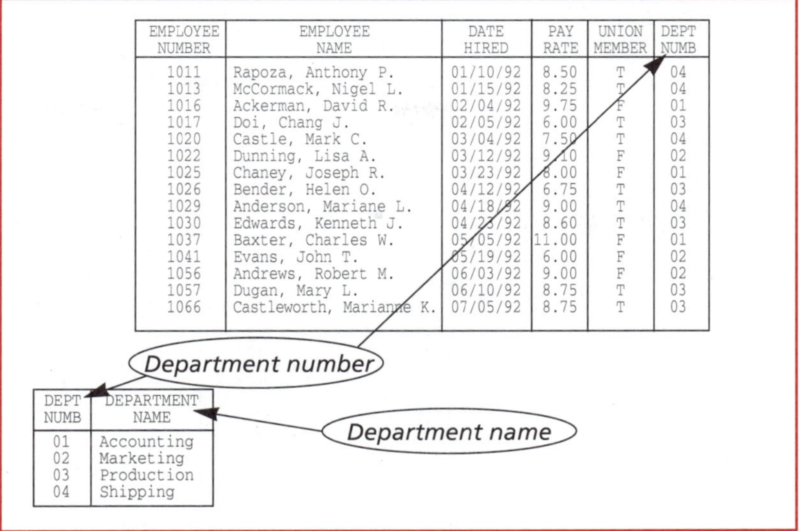

EMPLOYEE NUMBER	EMPLOYEE NAME	DATE HIRED	PAY RATE	UNION MEMBER	DEPT NUMB
1011	Rapoza, Anthony P.	01/10/92	8.50	T	04
1013	McCormack, Nigel L.	01/15/92	8.25	T	04
1016	Ackerman, David R.	02/04/92	9.75	F	01
1017	Doi, Chang J.	02/05/92	6.00	T	03
1020	Castle, Mark C.	03/04/92	7.50	T	04
1022	Dunning, Lisa A.	03/12/92	9.10	F	02
1025	Chaney, Joseph R.	03/23/92	8.00	F	01
1026	Bender, Helen O.	04/12/92	6.75	T	03
1029	Anderson, Mariane L.	04/18/92	9.00	T	04
1030	Edwards, Kenneth J.	04/23/92	8.60	T	03
1037	Baxter, Charles W.	05/05/92	11.00	F	01
1041	Evans, John T.	05/19/92	6.00	F	02
1056	Andrews, Robert M.	06/03/92	9.00	F	02
1057	Dugan, Mary L.	06/10/92	8.75	T	03
1066	Castleworth, Marianne K.	07/05/92	8.75	T	03

DEPT NUMB	DEPARTMENT NAME
01	Accounting
02	Marketing
03	Production
04	Shipping

TIP You will have problems with any reports or screens that included the field that you just deleted. Thus you should be sure to modify such reports or screens and remove the field from them.

thousand records? It would take a long time to make these changes, with many chances to make errors. Fortunately there is an easier way. You can use update queries.

Deleting a Field 159

If a field is no longer necessary, there is no point in leaving it in the database file. You are better off deleting it. ◀

TUTORIAL

In this tutorial, you change the structure of the database from the one represented in Figure 18.1 to the one represented in Figure 18.2. In particular, you will:

1. Change the length of the NAME field in the EMPLOYEE database file to 24.
2. Add the DEPT_NUMB field to the EMPLOYEE file.
3. Fill in the DEPT_NUMB field with appropriate values.
4. Delete the DEPARTMENT field from the EMPLOYEE database file.

1 Change the width of the NAME field in the EMPLOYEE database file to 24.

Select	EMPLOYEE	from Data column of Control Center.
Select	"Modify structure/order"	

You are taken to the Database Design screen. The Organize menu is on the screen.

Press	ESC	Removes Organize menu.

Your screen should now look like Figure 18.3. Note that your current structure is displayed.

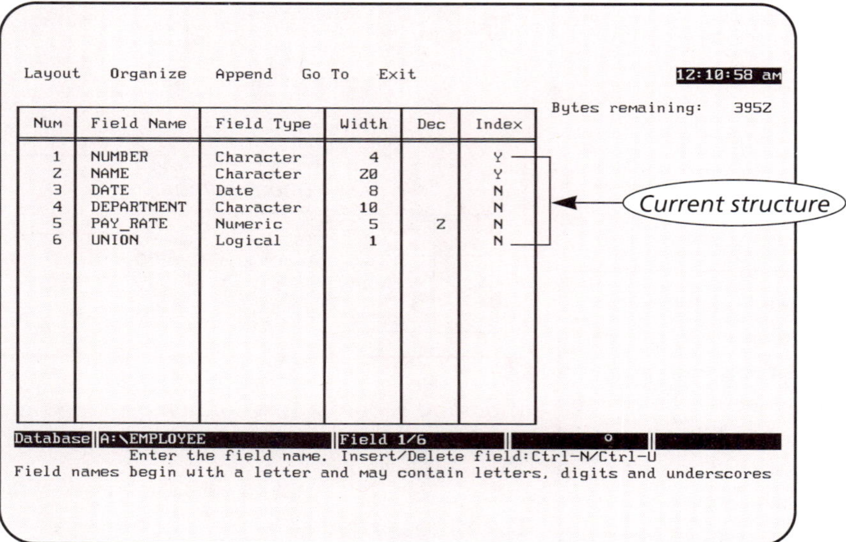

Figure 18.3
Database Design Screen

Press	↓	Highlights NAME field.
Press	↵ ENTER twice	Moves to Width column.
Type	24	
Press	↵ ENTER	Changes width.
Select	"Save changes and exit"	From Exit menu.
Press	↵ ENTER	Confirms that you are done.

The line at the bottom of your screen states that "Database records will be APPENDED from backup fields of the same name only!!" This simply means that, if you changed the name of any field, dBASE would not be able to keep the current data. Since you did not do so, there is no problem.

2 Add the DEPT_NUMB field to the EMPLOYEE database file. It should be a CHARACTER field, have a width of 2, and be the last field in the database file.

Select	EMPLOYEE	from Data column of Control Center.
Select	"Modify structure/order"	

Press	ESC	Removes Organize menu.
Press	↓ six times	Moves past last field.

A new line is created.

Type	DEPT_NUMB	
Press	↵ ENTER	Names new field.
Press	↵ ENTER	Selects Character as type.
Type	2	
Press	↵ ENTER	Enters field width.
Press	Y	Indicates field is to be indexed.
Select	"Save changes and exit"	from Exit menu.
Press	↵ ENTER	Confirms that you are done.

Once the process is complete, your database looks like Figure 18.4. Note the new field, DEPT_NUMB, on the right. No entries have yet been filled in for DEPT_NUMB. Note also that the NAME field is wider than it was before.

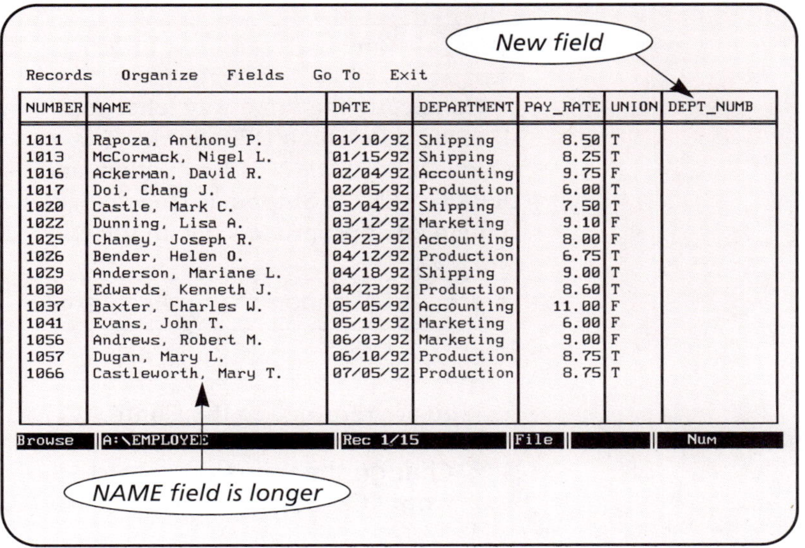

NUMBER	NAME	DATE	DEPARTMENT	PAY_RATE	UNION	DEPT_NUMB
1011	Rapoza, Anthony P.	01/10/92	Shipping	8.50	T	
1013	McCormack, Nigel L.	01/15/92	Shipping	8.25	T	
1016	Ackerman, David R.	02/04/92	Accounting	9.75	F	
1017	Doi, Chang J.	02/05/92	Production	6.00	T	
1020	Castle, Mark C.	03/04/92	Shipping	7.50	T	
1022	Dunning, Lisa A.	03/12/92	Marketing	9.10	F	
1025	Chaney, Joseph R.	03/23/92	Accounting	8.00	F	
1026	Bender, Helen O.	04/12/92	Production	6.75	T	
1029	Anderson, Mariane L.	04/18/92	Shipping	9.00	T	
1030	Edwards, Kenneth J.	04/23/92	Production	8.60	T	
1037	Baxter, Charles W.	05/05/92	Accounting	11.00	F	
1041	Evans, John T.	05/19/92	Marketing	6.00	F	
1056	Andrews, Robert M.	06/03/92	Marketing	9.00	F	
1057	Dugan, Mary L.	06/10/92	Production	8.75	T	
1066	Castleworth, Mary T.	07/05/92	Production	8.75	T	

Figure 18.4
Browse Screen

3 Make the entries for the DEPT_NUMB field using update queries.

Activate	EMPLOYEE	unless already active.

Select	<create>	in Queries column.
Select	"Specify update operation"	from Update menu.
Select	"Replace values in Employee.dbf"	

You are asked if you want to proceed with update query.

Select	"Proceed"	
Press	TAB four times	Moves to DEPARTMENT column.
Type	"Accounting"	
Press	↵ ENTER	Completes condition.
Press	TAB three times	Moves to DEPT_NUMB column.
Type	WITH "01"	
Press	↵ ENTER	Completes replacement expression.
Select	"Perform the update"	from Update menu.

At this point, the update takes place and you see a message indicating that three records have been replaced.

Press	(any key)	Removes message.

In exactly the same way, change the value for DEPT_NUMB to 02 for all records in which DEPARTMENT is Marketing, 03 for all records in which DEPARTMENT is Production, and 04 for all records in which DEPARTMENT is Shipping. The changes are then complete and all records contain an appropriate value in the DEPT_NUMB field.

Select	"Abandon changes and exit"	from Exit menu.
Select	"Yes"	Abandons query.

You are returned to the Control Center.

4 Change the name on record 15 of the EMPLOYEE database file from "Castleworth, Mary T." to "Castleworth, Marianne K.".

Activate	EMPLOYEE	unless already active.
Press	F2 once or twice	Moves to Edit screen.
Press	PAGE UP or PAGE DOWN (as necessary)	Moves to record 15.

You could also use the Go To menu to move to record 15.

Press	↵ ENTER	Moves to NAME field.
Type	Castleworth, Marianne K.	Changes name.
Select	"Exit"	from Exit menu.

You are returned to the Control Center. Your database now contains the data shown in Figure 18.5. Note that the DEPT_NUMB column contains the correct values and that Marianne Castleworth's name is now correct.

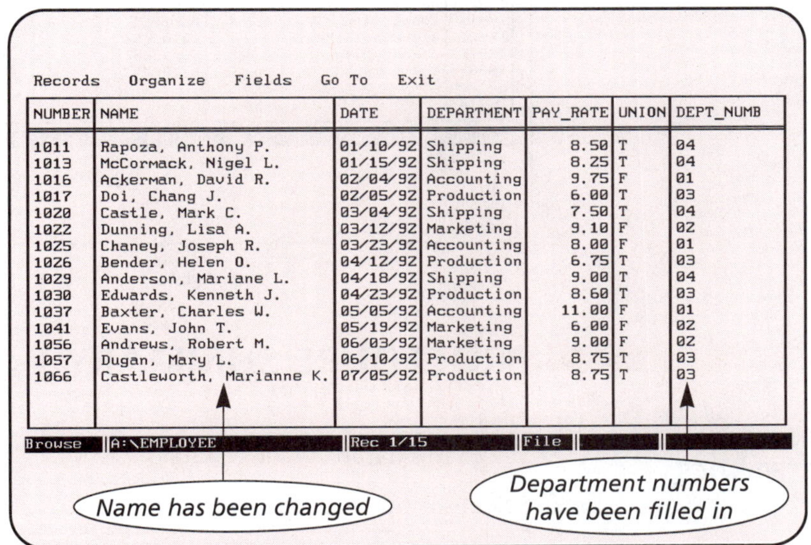

NUMBER	NAME	DATE	DEPARTMENT	PAY_RATE	UNION	DEPT_NUMB
1011	Rapoza, Anthony P.	01/10/92	Shipping	8.50	T	04
1013	McCormack, Nigel L.	01/15/92	Shipping	8.25	T	04
1016	Ackerman, David R.	02/04/92	Accounting	9.75	F	01
1017	Doi, Chang J.	02/05/92	Production	6.00	T	03
1020	Castle, Mark C.	03/04/92	Shipping	7.50	T	04
1022	Dunning, Lisa A.	03/12/92	Marketing	9.10	F	02
1025	Chaney, Joseph R.	03/23/92	Accounting	8.00	F	01
1026	Bender, Helen O.	04/12/92	Production	6.75	T	03
1029	Anderson, Mariane L.	04/18/92	Shipping	9.00	T	04
1030	Edwards, Kenneth J.	04/23/92	Production	8.60	T	03
1037	Baxter, Charles W.	05/05/92	Accounting	11.00	F	01
1041	Evans, John T.	05/19/92	Marketing	6.00	F	02
1056	Andrews, Robert M.	06/03/92	Marketing	9.00	F	02
1057	Dugan, Mary L.	06/10/92	Production	8.75	T	03
1066	Castleworth, Marianne K.	07/05/92	Production	8.75	T	03

Figure 18.5
Browse Screen

5 Delete the DEPARTMENT field from the EMPLOYEE database file.

Select	EMPLOYEE	from Data column of Control Center.
Select	"Modify structure/order"	
Press	ESC	Removes Organize menu.
Press	↓ three times	Moves to DEPARTMENT field.
Press	CTRL-U	Removes DEPARTMENT field.
Select	"Save changes and exit"	from Exit menu.
Press	↵ ENTER	Confirms that you are done.

Your database now contains the data shown in Figure 18.6. Note that there is no DEPARTMENT column.

Figure 18.6
Browse Screen

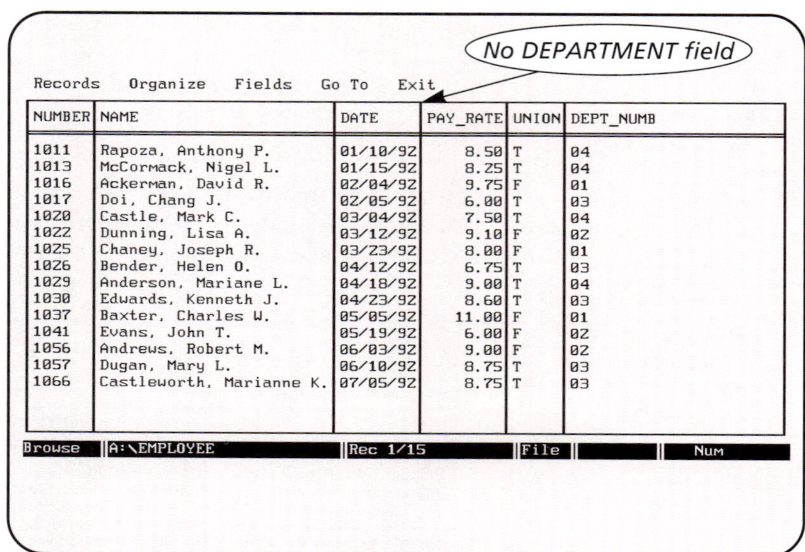

NUMBER	NAME	DATE	PAY_RATE	UNION	DEPT_NUMB
1011	Rapoza, Anthony P.	01/10/92	8.50	T	04
1013	McCormack, Nigel L.	01/15/92	8.25	T	04
1016	Ackerman, David R.	02/04/92	9.75	F	01
1017	Doi, Chang J.	02/05/92	6.00	T	03
1020	Castle, Mark C.	03/04/92	7.50	T	04
1022	Dunning, Lisa A.	03/12/92	9.10	F	02
1025	Chaney, Joseph R.	03/23/92	8.00	F	01
1026	Bender, Helen O.	04/12/92	6.75	T	03
1029	Anderson, Mariane L.	04/18/92	9.00	T	04
1030	Edwards, Kenneth J.	04/23/92	8.60	T	03
1037	Baxter, Charles W.	05/05/92	11.00	F	01
1041	Evans, John T.	05/19/92	6.00	F	02
1056	Andrews, Robert M.	06/03/92	9.00	F	02
1057	Dugan, Mary L.	06/10/92	8.75	T	03
1066	Castleworth, Marianne K.	07/05/92	8.75	T	03

PROCEDURE SUMMARY

CHANGING FIELD CHARACTERISTICS

Select the database file.	(your choice)
Select "Modify structure/order."	
Remove the Organize menu.	ESC
Highlight the field to be changed.	↓
Highlight the information to be changed.	↵ ENTER
Type the new entry.	(your input)
Select "Save changes and exit" from the Exit menu.	
Confirm that you are done.	↵ ENTER

ADDING A NEW FIELD

Select the database file.	(your choice)
Select "Modify structure/order."	
Remove the Organize menu.	ESC
Move the highlight to the position where you want to add the new field.	↓

If the new field is to be added at the end, you are ready to type the contents for the field. If not, make room for the field.	CTRL - N
Make the entries for the new field.	(your input)
Select "Save changes and exit" from the Exit menu.	
Confirm that you are done.	↵ ENTER

DELETING A FIELD

Select the database file.	(your choice)
Select "Modify structure/order."	
Remove the Organize menu.	ESC
Highlight the field to be deleted.	↓
Delete the field.	CTRL - U
Select "Save changes and exit" from the Exit menu.	
Confirm that you are done.	↵ ENTER

EXERCISES

The structure of the CHECK database file is to be changed from:

CHECKNUM	DATE	PAYEE	AMOUNT	EXPENSE	TAXDED
109	01/19/92	Oak Apartments	750.00	Household	Y
102	01/05/92	Sav-Mor Groceries	85.00	Food	N
106	01/12/92	Performing Arts	25.00	Charity	Y

.
.
.

to:

CHECKNUM	DATE	PAYEE	AMOUNT	TAXDED	EXP_CODE
109	01/19/92	Oak Apartments	750.00	Y	HH
102	01/05/92	Sav-Mor Groceries	85.00	N	FD
106	01/12/92	Performing Arts	25.00	Y	CH

.
.
.

EXP_CODE	EXPENSE
HH	Household
FD	Food
CH	Charity
AU	Automobile
EN	Entertainment
PR	Personal

1. Change the length of the PAYEE field in the CHECK database file to accommodate "Oakside View Apartments," which is the correct name for the PAYEE for check 109. Then make the change in the data.
2. Add the EXP_CODE field to the CHECK database.
3. Fill in the EXP_CODE field in the CHECK database with appropriate data (HH on records where EXPENSE is Household, FD on records where EXPENSE is Food, and so on).
4. Delete the EXPENSE field from the CHECK database.

Views (Using Multiple Database Files)

> **TIP** This discussion considers only those views involving two database files. The issues involving views with three or more database files are similar.

CONCEPTS

To access data from more than one database file in dBASE, you use a view. A **view** is a pseudo-database file that can combine two (or more) existing database files. (Saying it is a pseudo-database file simply means it appears to the user to be a database file, even though, in fact, it might not be.) The key points of this definition are:

1. By using views, you can access data from two or more database files at the same time.
2. Even though the data comes from more than one database file, it still feels as though it were a single database file. This makes working with a view much simpler than if you had to be concerned with all the individual database files that are involved in the view. ◀

To see how views work, consider the two database files shown in Figure 19.1, the EMPLOYEE file and the DEPT file. The database files are related through **matching fields**. In the figure, the matching fields are the DEPT_NUMB fields in both database files.

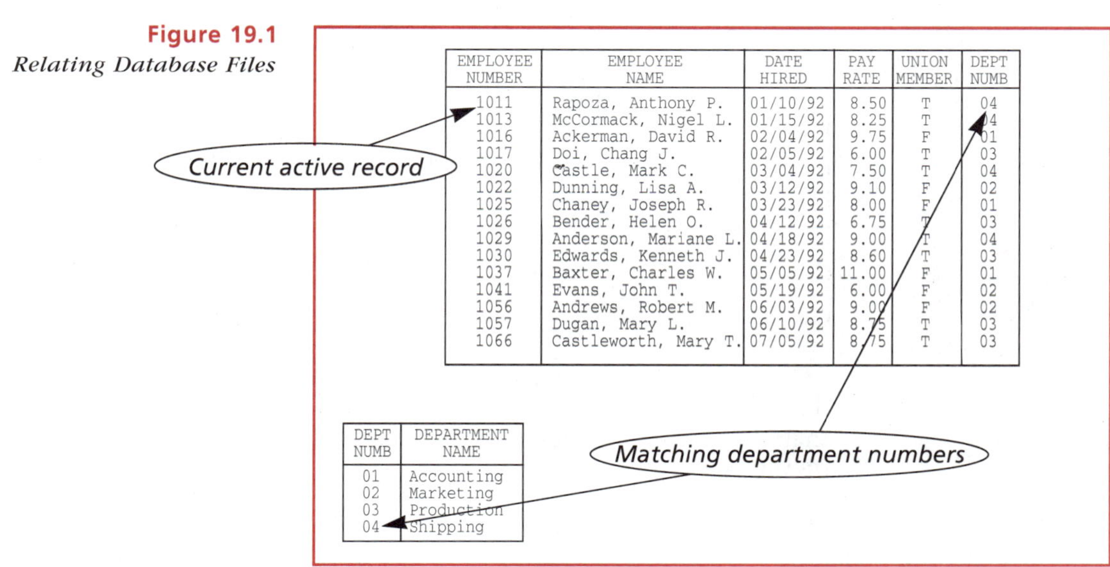

EMPLOYEE NUMBER	EMPLOYEE NAME	DATE HIRED	PAY RATE	UNION MEMBER	DEPT NUMB
1011	Rapoza, Anthony P.	01/10/92	8.50	T	04
1013	McCormack, Nigel L.	01/15/92	8.25	T	04
1016	Ackerman, David R.	02/04/92	9.75	F	01
1017	Doi, Chang J.	02/05/92	6.00	T	03
1020	Castle, Mark C.	03/04/92	7.50	T	04
1022	Dunning, Lisa A.	03/12/92	9.10	F	02
1025	Chaney, Joseph R.	03/23/92	8.00	F	01
1026	Bender, Helen O.	04/12/92	6.75	T	03
1029	Anderson, Mariane L.	04/18/92	9.00	T	04
1030	Edwards, Kenneth J.	04/23/92	8.60	T	03
1037	Baxter, Charles W.	05/05/92	11.00	F	01
1041	Evans, John T.	05/19/92	6.00	F	02
1056	Andrews, Robert M.	06/03/92	9.00	F	02
1057	Dugan, Mary L.	06/10/92	8.75	T	03
1066	Castleworth, Mary T.	07/05/92	8.75	T	03

DEPT NUMB	DEPARTMENT NAME
01	Accounting
02	Marketing
03	Production
04	Shipping

Figure 19.1
Relating Database Files

A special kind of relationship, called a **one-to-many relationship**, exists between these two files. In this case, a department is associated with *many* employees, but each employee is associated with only *one* department. Looking at the values, for example, you can see that Department 01 (Accounting), for example, is associated with employees 1016, 1025, 1037, and 1070. Employee 1016, on the other hand, is associated with *only* the Accounting department. In this relationship, you would refer to DEPT as the "one" database file and to EMPLOYEE as the "many" database file.

When two database files are related in this fashion, they can become part of a view. In such a case, you work with the "many" database file and dBASE automatically keeps track of which record in the "one" file is associated with the current active record in this "many" file. For example, if record 1 (employee 1011) is the current active record, dBASE knows that the related record in the DEPT file is record 4 (department 04) since the department numbers match (see the arrow in Figure 19.1). dBASE allows you to use not only fields in the EMPLOYEE file, but also any fields in the DEPT file. Thus, if you list the department name for employee 1011, you will get Shipping because it is the name on the related record in the DEPT file. Suppose you make record 3 the current active record (Figure 19.2). Then the corresponding record in the DEPT file is record 1 (department 01). If you list the department name for this employee, you will get Accounting.

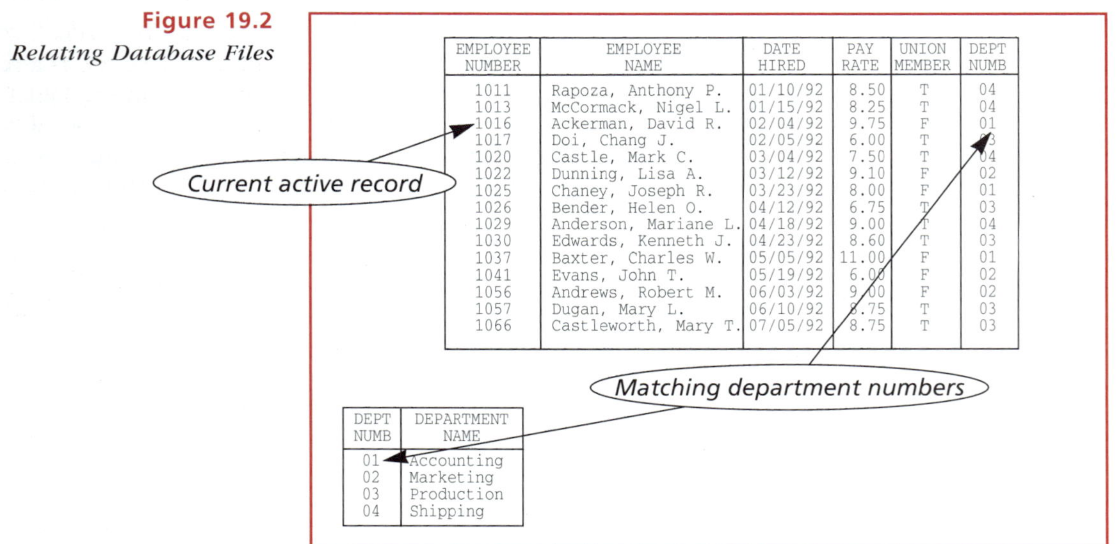

EMPLOYEE NUMBER	EMPLOYEE NAME	DATE HIRED	PAY RATE	UNION MEMBER	DEPT NUMB
1011	Rapoza, Anthony P.	01/10/92	8.50	T	04
1013	McCormack, Nigel L.	01/15/92	8.25	T	04
1016	Ackerman, David R.	02/04/92	9.75	F	01
1017	Doi, Chang J.	02/05/92	6.00	T	03
1020	Castle, Mark C.	03/04/92	7.50	T	04
1022	Dunning, Lisa A.	03/12/92	9.10	F	02
1025	Chaney, Joseph R.	03/23/92	8.00	F	01
1026	Bender, Helen O.	04/12/92	6.75	T	03
1029	Anderson, Mariane L.	04/18/92	9.00	T	04
1030	Edwards, Kenneth J.	04/23/92	8.60	T	03
1037	Baxter, Charles W.	05/05/92	11.00	F	01
1041	Evans, John T.	05/19/92	6.00	F	02
1056	Andrews, Robert M.	06/03/92	9.00	F	02
1057	Dugan, Mary L.	06/10/92	8.75	T	03
1066	Castleworth, Mary T.	07/05/92	8.75	T	03

DEPT NUMB	DEPARTMENT NAME
01	Accounting
02	Marketing
03	Production
04	Shipping

Figure 19.2
Relating Database Files

When accessing such a view, you do not have to be aware of these details. dBASE handles them for you automatically. You simply indicate that you want to include the department name on a display or report, and dBASE ensures that it is the correct name.

> **TIP** To make working with the view as efficient as possible, it is a good idea to make sure that there are indexes for the fields in the database files that will be used to link the files.

Preparing for View Creation

164

Before you begin creating a view, you should decide exactly which database files are to be included. You should also decide how they are related; that is, which database file is the "one" and which is the "many." In addition, you need to determine the fields that will be used to link the database files. ◄

TUTORIAL

In this tutorial, you determine all the information necessary to create the view of departments and employees. You also create the DEPT database file.

1 Create a view of departments and employees called EMPDEPT. Identify the database files involved in the view. Determine which one is the "one" and which one is the "many." Decide which fields will be used to relate the files; that is, determine the matching fields. Make sure indexes exist on these fields.

- The database files are EMPLOYEE and DEPT (employees and departments).
- DEPT is the "one" and EMPLOYEE is the "many." (A department is related to *many* employees, but an employee is related to only *one* department.)
- The DEPT_NUMB fields in both database files are used to relate the files. The DEPT_NUMB field in the EMPLOYEE database file is already indexed. Make sure you index the DEPT_NUMB field in the DEPT database file when you create the file.

2 Create the DEPT database file. The DEPT_NUMB field should be indexed.

Select	<create>	in Data column of Control Center.
Type	DEPT_NUMB	
Press	↵ ENTER	Names first field.
Press	↵ ENTER	Selects Character as field type.
Type	2	
Press	↵ ENTER	Enters field width.
Press	Y	Field is indexed.
Type	DEPARTMENT	Names second field.
Press	↵ ENTER	Selects Character as field type.

Type	10	
Press	↵ ENTER	Enters field width.
Press	N	Field is not indexed.
Select	"Save changes and exit"	from Exit menu.
Type	DEPT	Names database file.
Select	"Change description of highlighted file"	from Catalog menu.
Type	Department database file	Describes file.

Then enter the data that is shown in Figure 19.3. (The first record has 01 for a department number and Accounting for a department name; the second record has 02 for a number and Marketing for a name; and so on. Make sure to enter the zeros in the department number field.)

Select	"Exit"	from Exit menu.

You are returned to the Control Center.

Figure 19.3
Data for DEPT Database File

Record#	DEPT_NUMB	DEPARTMENT
1	01	Accounting
2	02	Marketing
3	03	Production
4	04	Shipping

PROCEDURE SUMMARY

PREPARING FOR VIEW CREATION

Identify the database files that will be used in the view.	
Determine how the files are related; that is, determine which is the "many" file and which is the "one" file.	
Decide which fields will be used to link (relate) the files.	
Be sure both database files already exist. If either one does not, create it.	(your input)
Make sure the fields used for linking the database files are both indexed.	

EXERCISES

1. Create the new database file (the file of expense codes and descriptions shown in the exercises in the previous topic). Use the name EXPCATS for this file. The EXP_CODE field should be indexed.
2. Add the indicated expense codes and descriptions to this database file.
3. You are to create a view called EXPVIEW. This view should contain both the EXPCATS and the CHECK database files. The EXP_CODE field in both files should be used to relate the two. Include all fields from the CHECK database and the expense description field from the EXPCATS database in this view. Use this information to determine the database files to be included. Determine which is the "many" database file and which is the "one" database file.

Creating Views

CONCEPTS

In dBASE, you use the same Query Design screen you saw earlier to create views. In simplest terms, a view is just a *saved query*; that is, dBASE considers any query you save to be a view. Thus all you need to do is create an appropriate query and save it.

Beginning the View Creation Process 170

To begin the view creation process, you must have identified the database files and the relationship between them. Then you are ready to begin creating the view. The real benefits come, of course, once the view has been created and you can begin using it.

Relating the Database Files 171

As part of the view creation process, you must indicate to dBASE how the database files in the view are related; that is, you must indicate the matching fields. Once you have indicated this relationship, dBASE handles it automatically for you whenever you use the view. You can be assured that when you use fields from more than one database file, the data will "match." For example, if you list an employee's name (from the EMPLOYEE file), department number (from the EMPLOYEE file), and also department name (from the DEPT file), you know that dBASE will list the appropriate department name.

Selecting Fields 171

You are not required to include all the fields from all the database files in a view. If you know you will not need certain fields, you can simplify the view by not including them. At this point in the process, you indicate which fields from the database files you want to include in the view.

Finishing the View Creation Process 171

To finish the process, all you need to do is save the query. In the process you will give the saved query a name. You have now created your view.

TUTORIAL

In this tutorial, you create the view of departments and employees. You do it by first creating an appropriate query and then saving the query as EMPDEPT (the name you will give to the view).

1 **Create a query containing the EMPLOYEE and DEPT database files.** This begins the creation of the EMPDEPT view.

Activate	EMPLOYEE	unless already active.
Select	<create>	from Queries column.

As you have seen, the use of indexes can greatly improve efficiency. dBASE uses indexes in queries and views, but only if you indicate that indexes are to be included.

Select	"Include indexes"	from Fields menu.

This changes the "no" to "yes" so that dBASE will include indexes. (You won't see the change because the menu disappears.) Your screen should now look like Figure 20.1. The number sign (#) preceding NUMBER indicates that there is an index on the NUMBER field that dBASE can use. Note that a number sign is not in front of DATE because you did not create an index for DATE. So far only the EMPLOYEE file is included in your query. You also need to include the DEPT file.

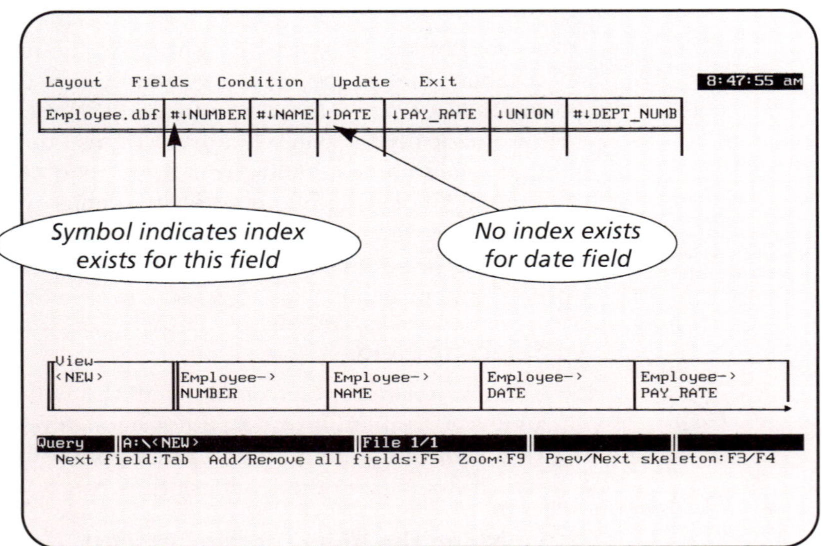

Figure 20.1
Query Design Screen

Select	"Add file to query"	from Layout menu.

You are presented with a list of possible files.

Select	DEPT	Adds DEPT file to query.

Now you need to include indexes for the DEPT file.

Select	"Include indexes"	from Fields menu.

Do not save your work at this point. Instead proceed directly to the next task.

TIP Each time you press F4 you move to the next skeleton on the screen. If you're on the last skeleton, the View skeleton, you'll move back to the first one, the skeleton for EMPLOYEE.

2 **Relate the database files in the query.** You need to relate the files; that is, you need to indicate the fields that will be used to link them.

Press	F3	Moves to EMPLOYEE skeleton.

You could also use F4. ◀

Press	TAB six times	Moves to DEPT_NUMB column.
Select	"Create link by pointing"	from Layout menu.

dBASE inserts LINK1 in the column in which your cursor is positioned. A message instructs you to move the cursor to the other field in the linking process and then to press Enter.

Press	F4	Moves to DEPT skeleton.
Press	TAB	Moves to DEPT_NUMB column.
Press	↵ ENTER	Completes link.

At this point, your screen should look like Figure 20.2. Note that both DEPT_NUMB columns now include LINK1. This is the way dBASE indicates that these are the fields it will use to link the two files. Do not save your work at this point. Instead proceed directly to the next task.

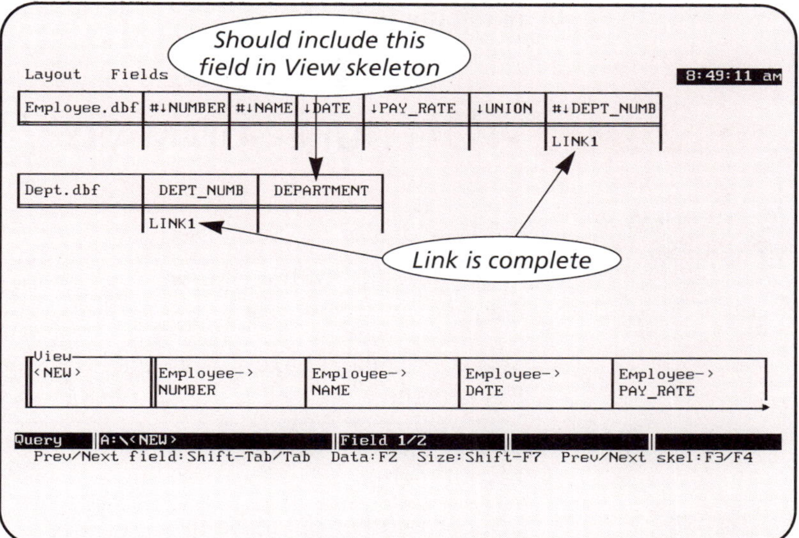

Figure 20.2
Query Design Screen

3 **Specify the fields to be included in the query.** When you are done, save the query, thus creating a view. You now have included both files, and you have linked them. The View skeleton has not changed, however; it still includes only fields from EMPLOYEE. You don't need to include the DEPT_NUMB field in DEPT because this field should exactly match the DEPT_NUMB field in EMPLOYEE, which is already included in the View skeleton. You should include DEPARTMENT, however.

Press	TAB	Moves to DEPARTMENT column.
Press	F5	Includes column in skeleton.

Next you remove the DEPT_NUMB field from the skeleton.

Press	F3	Moves to EMPLOYEE skeleton.

The cursor should be in the DEPT_NUMB column.

Press	F5	Removes field from skeleton.
Select	"Save changes and exit"	from Exit menu.
Type	EMPDEPT	
Press	↵ ENTER	Names query.

You have now saved your query as EMPDEPT. Thus you have effectively created a view and called it EMPDEPT. (Remember that a view is the same as a saved query.) Your view will be displayed in the Queries column of the Control Center.

PROCEDURE SUMMARY

BEGINNING THE VIEW CREATION PROCESS

Activate one of the database files.	(your choice)
Select <create> in the Queries column.	
Select "Include indexes" from the Fields menu.	
Select "Add file to query" from the Layout menu.	
Select the other database file.	(your choice)
Select "Include indexes" from the Fields menu.	

RELATING THE DATABASE FILES

Move to the skeleton for the first database file.	F3
Move to the linking field.	TAB (as necessary)
Select "Create link by pointing" from the Layout menu.	
Move to the skeleton for the second database file.	F4
Move to the linking field.	TAB (as necessary)
Complete the link.	↵ ENTER

SELECTING FIELDS

To add a field to the View skeleton:

Move to the File skeleton containing the field you want to add.	F3 or F4 (as necessary)
Move to the field you want to add.	TAB or SHIFT-TAB (as necessary)
Add the field.	F5

To remove a field from the View skeleton:

Move to the File skeleton containing the field you want to remove.	F3 or F4 (as necessary)
Move to the field you want to remove.	TAB or SHIFT-TAB (as necessary)
Remove the field.	F5

FINISHING THE VIEW CREATION PROCESS

Select "Save changes and exit" from the Exit menu.	
Enter the name of the saved query (view).	(your input), ↵ ENTER

EXERCISES

1. Begin the process of creating EXPVIEW. Create a query containing the appropriate database files.
2. Indicate to dBASE how the database files in the query are to be related.
3. Specify the fields that are to be included in the query. Save the query as EXPVIEW.

TOPIC 21

Using Views

CONCEPTS

Now that you have created your view, you can realize the benefits from it. Whenever you want to combine data from the various database files in the view, all you need to do is use the view. You can use it with retrieval options like "List" and "Display." You can also use it in reports and labels. In both cases, you use it just as though it were a single database file.

Using a View

177

Once you have created a view, you can begin to use it. To do so, you simply need to activate it. dBASE handles all the necessary details. The use of views, however, involves some special considerations:

1. To update any of the data, update the appropriate database file. For example, to add a new employee, activate the EMPLOYEE database file and use the "Add new records" option on the Edit or Browse screen. To change the name of an employee, activate the EMPLOYEE database file and use the Edit or Browse screen. To add a new department, on the other hand, activate the DEPT database file before you use the "Add new records" option.
2. The data never exists in the form represented in a view. Rather, dBASE draws data from the underlying database files and assembles it in the appropriate form *at the time you access the view*. No special action is taken beforehand. The nice thing about this arrangement is that, whenever changes are made to any of the database files that are included in the view, you automatically see the results of these changes the next time you use the view. You don't need to re-create the view in order to access the current data.

Sorting a View or Query

Sometimes you might want the data as defined in your view, but you would like it in a different order. Thus you need to be able to sort the data in your view. Since a view is just a saved query, the same techniques apply equally well to sorting the output of a query.

TUTORIAL

In this tutorial, you use the view you have created.

1 **List all the records in the EMPDEPT view.** If you just created the view, it is still active. It appears above the line in the Queries column. If it is not, you must activate it.

Select	EMPDEPT	in Queries column.
Select	"Use view"	Activates view.

The view is now active. Any subsequent options such as using the Browse screen or producing a report will use this view.

Press	F2 once or twice	Moves to Browse screen.

You now see the data in your view. If you wish to print a report of all the data, you could use Quick Report (Shift-F9).

2 Using the EMPDEPT view, list the number, name, and department of all employees hired after March 1, 1992.

Select	EMPDEPT	in Queries column.
Select	"Modify query"	Moves to Query Design screen.

The query you created for your view is displayed. You can now make appropriate changes to it and then press F2 to see the results of your new query. You need to change your View skeleton to contain NUMBER and NAME from the EMPLOYEE skeleton and DEPARTMENT from the DEPT skeleton. Your highlight should be under Employee.dbf. If it is not, use F3 or F4 to move to the EMPLOYEE skeleton and then Tab or Shift-Tab to move the highlight under Employee.dbf.

TIP It's very easy to tell how many times you should press F5. Just look at the View skeleton, and press F5 until the fields disappear.

Press	F5 twice	Removes all EMPLOYEE fields from skeleton.

In this example, you had to press F5 twice. In other situations, you may need to press it only once. ◄

Press	F4	Moves to DEPT skeleton.

If the highlight is not under Dept.dbf, use Tab or Shift-Tab to get it there.

Press	F5 twice	Removes all fields from View skeleton.

In this case, you need to press F5 twice. The first time you press F5, *all* fields from DEPT are included in the skeleton because they're not already there; the second time, they are removed.

Press	F3	Moves to EMPLOYEE skeleton.
Press	TAB	Moves to NUMBER field.
Press	F5	Adds NUMBER field to View skeleton.

Press	TAB	Moves to NAME field.
Press	F5	Adds NAME field to View skeleton.
Press	F4	Moves to DEPT skeleton.
Press	TAB twice	Moves to DEPARTMENT field.
Press	F5	Adds DEPARTMENT field to View skeleton.

The View skeleton is now correct. The final step is to enter the condition.

Press	F3	Moves to EMPLOYEE skeleton.
Press	TAB	Moves to DATE field.
Type	>{3/01/92}	
Press	↵ ENTER	Completes condition.
Press	F2	Applies query.
Select	"Exit"	from Exit menu.

Since you changed the definition of a query, dBASE asks you if you want to save it. *Be sure you answer no*. Saving it would replace the old definition with this new one!

Select	"No"	Does not replace query.

3 **Display all the data in the EMPDEPT view.** The data is to be sorted by name.

Select	EMPDEPT	in Queries column.
Select	"Modify query"	Moves to Query Design screen.

Use F3, F4, Tab, or Shift-Tab, if necessary, to move the highlight under Employee.dbf.

Press	TAB twice	Moves to NAME field.
Select	"Sort on this field"	from Fields menu.

You then see the same list of possible sort types you saw when you sorted a database file.

Select	"Ascending ASCII"	Selects sort type.

Your screen should now look like Figure 21.1. The entry Asc1 in the NAME field indicates two things. First, the abbreviation Asc is the dBASE code for Ascending ASCII. Second, the number 1 indicates that this is the first sort field. This number only becomes meaningful if you have more than one sort field.

Figure 21.1
Query Design Screen

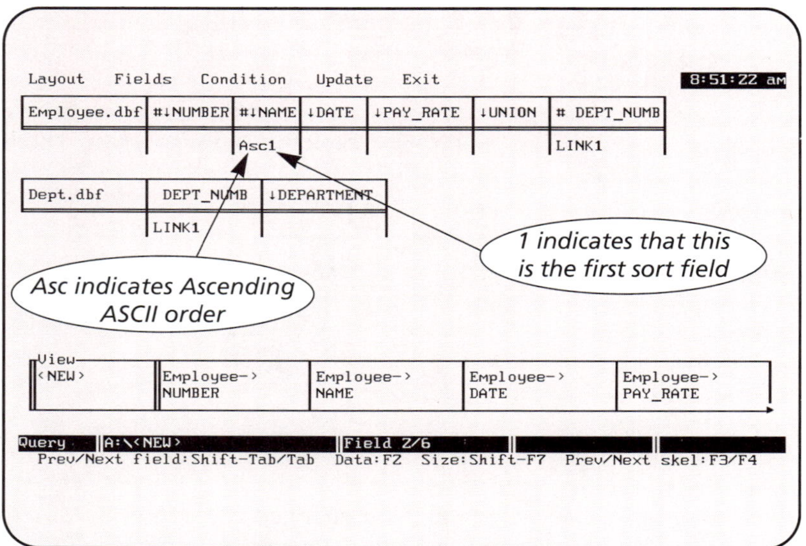

Press	F2	Applies query.

Your data should be sorted by NAME.

Select	"Exit"	from Exit menu.
Select	"No"	Does not replace query.

4 **Display all the data in the EMPDEPT view.** The data is to be sorted by name within department.

Select	EMPDEPT	in Queries column.
Select	"Modify query"	Moves to Query Design screen.

Use F3, F4, Tab, or Shift-Tab, if necessary, to move the highlight under Employee.dbf. Select the sort keys in order of importance. Since DEPARTMENT is the more important of the two, you must select it first.

Press	F4	Moves highlight to DEPT.

Your cursor should be in the DEPARTMENT field. If it is not, press Tab to move it there.

Select	"Sort on this field"	from Fields menu.
Select	"Ascending ASCII"	Selects sort type.
Press	F3	Moves to EMPLOYEE.
Press	TAB twice	Moves to NAME field.
Select	"Sort on this field"	from Fields menu.
Select	"Ascending ASCII"	Selects sort type.

Note that the entry in the NAME column is Asc2. dBASE has assigned the next higher number. There is something important about this number, however. The present query has two Asc entries: Asc1 in the DEPARTMENT column and Asc2 in the NAME column. The column with the *smaller* number will be treated as the more important sort key. It doesn't matter what the specific numbers are, just which one is smaller. This is why it's important to select the more important key first.

Press	F2	Applies query.

Your data should be sorted by NAME within DEPARTMENT.

Select	"Exit"	from Exit menu.
Select	"No"	Does not replace query.

Although the preceding discussion explains how to sort views, remember that views are nothing more than stored queries. Thus, in the preceding discussion, you were also learning how to sort queries. The same techniques apply to sorting a query whether or not the query will ultimately be saved.

PROCEDURE SUMMARY

USING A VIEW

To use all the fields and records in the view:

Select the view in the Queries column.	(your choice)
Select "Use view."	

To restrict the records, restrict the fields, and/or sort the data in a view:

Select the view in the Queries column.	(your choice)
Select "Modify query."	
Take an appropriate action from among the following options.	

To restrict the records:

Enter a condition.	(your input)

To restrict the fields:

Move the beginning of the skeleton for the first database file.	F3 or F4 or TAB or SHIFT-TAB
Remove all fields from this database file.	F5
Move the beginning of the skeleton for the second database file.	F3 or F4 or TAB or SHIFT-TAB
Remove all fields from this database file.	F5
Add the desired fields to the View skeleton. (To add a field, move the highlight to it and then press F5.)	F3 or F4 or TAB or SHIFT-TAB, F5

To sort the data:

Move the highlight to the sort key. (If there are two sort keys, move the highlight to the more important sort key.)	F3 or F4 or TAB or SHIFT-TAB
Select "Sort on this field" from the Fields menu.	
Select the sort type.	(your choice)
If there are two sort keys, move the highlight to the less important sort key.	
Select "Sort on this field" from the Fields menu.	
Select the sort type.	(your choice)

EXERCISES

1. Using the EXPVIEW view, display the check number, date, payee, and amount for all checks.
2. Using this view, display the check number, date, payee, and amount for all checks on which the description is Household.
3. Using this view, display the check number, date, payee, and amount for all checks on which the description is Household. Sort the data by payee.

Checkpoint 3

What You Should Know

- ✓ Before you create a report, be sure to activate the database file.
- ✓ To create a report, highlight <create> in the Reports column of the Control Center and press ENTER.
- ✓ The various portions of a report (**page header**, **report intro**, **group intro**, **detail**, **group summary**, and **report summary**) are specified by making entries in the appropriate **bands** in the Report Design screen.
- ✓ To terminate the report creation process, select either "Save" (to save your work) or "Abandon" (to exit without saving your work) from the Exit menu.
- ✓ To print a report from the Control Center, highlight the report, press ENTER, and then select "Print report."
- ✓ To limit the records that will appear in a report, use a query.
- ✓ To change the layout of an existing report, highlight the report at the Control Center, press ENTER, and then select "Modify layout."
- ✓ To specify **grouping** on a report, add a **group band**.
- ✓ If you include subtotals in a report, you must make sure that the records are ordered appropriately before printing the report.
- ✓ To change the structure of a database file, highlight the database file at the Control Center, press ENTER, and select "Modify structure/order."
- ✓ To change the characteristics of a field, highlight the data to be changed and enter the new value.
- ✓ To add a field, highlight the beginning of the first row past all the existing fields, and then type in the name and characteristics of the new field.
- ✓ To make mass changes to the new field, use an update query.
- ✓ To delete a field, highlight the field to be deleted on the Database Design screen, hold the CONTROL key down, and type the letter U.
- ✓ In general terms, a **view** is a pseudo-table (or pseudo-database file). Although the same is true in dBASE, a view is specifically a saved query.
- ✓ A **one-to-many relationship** between two database files occurs when one record in one of the files is related to many records in the second, but each record in the second is related to only one record in the first. The first database file is called the *one* database file, and the second is called the *many* database file.
- ✓ To create a view, first create a query that describes exactly the database files, records, and fields you want in the view, and then save the query.

✓ To activate a view, highlight it at the Control Center, press ENTER, and then select "Use view."

✓ Once activated, a view may be used in displays and reports just as though it were a database file.

✓ To update any of the data in a view, update the appropriate database file.

Review Questions

1. How do you begin creating a report? How do you add a page title to a report?
2. How do you add columns to a report? How do you specify headings for the columns? How do you include a total in your report?
3. How do you print a report you have created, assuming you want all records included in the report?
4. How do you print a report you have created, assuming you only want certain records included in the report?
5. How do you include subtotals in a report? What is meant by grouping? What does it have to do with subtotals?
6. How do you print a report that includes subtotals? Are there any special issues concerning the records in the database file when you print such a report?
7. How do you change the characteristics of a field in a database file? Why might you want to do so?
8. How do you add a new field to a database file? Why might you want to do so?
9. How do you delete a field from a database file? Why might you want to do so?
10. What is a view? Why might you want to use one? What decisions should you make in preparation for creating a view?
11. How do you indicate to dBASE which database files are to be included in a view? How do you include indexes?
12. How do you indicate to dBASE how the database files in a view are related?
13. How do you indicate to dBASE which fields are to be included in a view?
14. How do you use a view once you have created one?

CHECKPOINT EXERCISES

1. Design a report for data in the MUSIC database file. The report is to contain page and column headings. Fields to be included on the report include the Category, Music Name, Artist Name, Type, and Cost. A final total of the Cost Amount field is to be displayed.

2. Begin the report creation process for this report. Call the report MUSRPT1. Correct the detail band.
3. Correct the report summary for MUSRPT1.
4. Correct the page header band for MUSRPT1.
5. Print a report of all records in the MUSIC database file. Use the report layout stored in MUSRPT1.
6. Print a report of those records in the MUSIC database file on which cost is less than $10.00. Use the report layout stored in MUSRPT1.
7. Modify the report format stored in MUSRPT1 so that a subtotal is taken when there is a change in category. Use this report format to display all the records in the MUSIC database file. Make sure that the records are ordered correctly.

The structure of the MUSIC database file is to be changed from:

DATE	NAME	ARTIST	TYPE	COST	CATEGORY
02/22/92	Greatest Hits	Panache, Milo	LP	8.95	Classical
02/15/92	America	Judd, Mary	CS	5.95	Vocal
01/02/92	Rio Rio	Duran, Ralph	LP	8.95	Rock

.
.
.

to:

DATE	NAME	ARTIST	TYPE	COST	CAT_CODE
02/22/92	Greatest Hits #1	Panache, Milo	LP	8.95	CL
02/15/92	America	Judd, Mary	CS	5.95	VO
01/02/92	Rio Rio	Duran, Ralph	LP	8.95	RK

.
.
.

CAT_CODE	CATEGORY
CL	Classical
CO	Country
VO	Vocal
RK	Rock

8. Change the length of the Name field in the MUSIC database file to accommodate "Greatest Hits #1," which is the correct name for the first record. Then make the change in the data.
9. Add the CAT_CODE field to the MUSIC database.
10. Fill in the CAT_CODE field in the MUSIC database with the appropriate data (CL on records where the category is Classical, CO on records where the category is Country, and so on).
11. Delete the Category field from the MUSIC database.
12. Create the new database file. Use the name MUSCATS for this file. The CAT_CODE field should be indexed.

13. Add the indicated category codes and descriptions to this database file.
14. Create a view called MUSVIEW. This view should contain both the MUSCATS and MUSIC database files. The CAT_CODE field in both files should be used to relate the two. Include all fields from the MUSIC database and the category description field from the MUSCATS database in this view.
15. Using this view, display the date, music name, artist, and cost for all classical records.
16. Using this view, display the date, music name, artist, and cost for all classical records. Sort the data by artist.

COMPREHENSIVE EXERCISE 1

You are to create a database file to store information about the inventory of a company that sells computer software. Fields in the database consist of the name of the software, the name of the company that sells the software, a software category, an entry T (true) or F (false) to indicate if the software is MS-DOS compatible, the quantity of software on hand, and the cost of the software. The software products in inventory are listed in the following chart.

SOFTWARE NAME	COMPANY	CATEGORY	MS_DOS	QUANTITY	COST
Databurst	Electric Software	Database	T	5	299.95
Type Ease	Edusoft Inc.	WP	F	22	29.95
Image Fonts	Graph Tech Inc.	WP	T	12	49.95
Data Filer	Anchor Software	Database	T	18	149.95
Master	Edusoft Inc.	Education	F	10	49.95
Math Tester	Learnit Software	Education	F	10	49.95
PC-Writer	Anchor Software	WP	T	30	129.95
Print File	Graph Tech Inc.	Database	T	16	99.95
Learning Calc	Edusoft Inc.	Spreadsheet	T	34	69.95
Number Crunch	Anchor Software	Spreadsheet	T	8	279.95

FIELD DESCRIPTION	FIELD NAME	FIELD TYPE	WIDTH	DECIMAL POSITIONS	INDEX
SOFTWARE NAME	NAME	CHARACTER	12		Y
COMPANY	COMPANY	CHARACTER	18		N
CATEGORY	CATEGORY	CHARACTER	12		N
MS_DOS	MS_DOS	LOGICAL	1		N
QUANTITY	QUANTITY	NUMERIC	4		N
COST	COST	NUMERIC	6	2	N

Perform the following tasks:

1. Insert your data disk into drive A. Then load dBASE.
2. Create a catalog called SOFTCAT.
3. Create the database file. Use the name SOFTWARE for the database file.
4. Enter the six fields in the preceding table.
5. Enter the preceding data. When you enter the third record, enter the name as Images Font and the price as $94.95.
6. After you have entered the records, enter an additional record. You may make up whatever entries you wish for the fields in this record.
7. Use SHIFT-F9 to print a list of all the data.
8. Correct the third record by changing the name to Image Fonts and the price to $49.95.
9. Delete the extra record that you added. Permanently remove the record from the database file.
10. Use SHIFT-F9 to print a list of all the data.
11. Make backup copies of this database file and the corresponding production index file. Call them SOFTBCK.DBF and SOFTBCK.MDX, respectively.
12. Activate the database file so that it can be accessed.

13. Display all the fields and all the records.
14. Display the Software Name field, the Category field, the MS-DOS field, the Quantity field, and the Cost field for all records in the database.
15. Display the Category field, the Software Name field, and the Cost field for all records in the database.
16. Display the record for the software called Image Fonts.
17. Display all software produced by the company Anchor Software.
18. Display all software with a category of Education.
19. Display all software that is MS-DOS compatible (the entry .T. in the MS-DOS field).
20. Display all records with a quantity less than 10.
21. Display all records with a quantity greater than 25.
22. Display all records in which the company name contains the word "Software."
23. Display all records in which the software name sounds like "Tipe."
24. Display all word processing software (WP in category field) that has a cost of less than $50.00.
25. Display all records with a category of Database or Spreadsheet.
26. Count the number of records in the database file.
27. Sum the quantity field to determine the number of products on hand.
28. Average the Cost field to determine the average cost of the software.
29. Average the cost of the software with a category of Education.
30. Average the cost of the software in each category.
31. Use the "Forward search" option to find the software named Data Filer.
32. Use the "Forward search" option to find the first record in the SOFTWARE database file that is in the WP category.
33. Use the appropriate option to locate the next record in the WP category.
34. Use the "Browse" option to change the cost of Math Tester to $59.95.
35. Use the "Browse" option to change the cost of Image Fonts to $54.95. In addition, change the category to Spreadsheet and change the quantity to 14.
36. Use an update query to change the cost of Print File to $104.95.
37. Use an update query to add $10.00 to the cost of all software in the Database category.
38. Use an update query to mark all software in the WP category for deletion.
39. Use an update query to unmark all software in the WP category.
40. Use the Edit screen to mark PC-Writer for deletion.
41. Use the Browse screen to mark Learning Calc for deletion.

42. Physically remove the marked records from the SOFTWARE database file.
43. List all the records in the SOFTWARE database file.
44. Create a form for the SOFTWARE database file that is similar to the form you created for the EMPLOYEE database file. Call it SOFTFORM.
45. Activate this form. Select the Edit screen to make sure the form is active. (Select the "Exit" option of the Exit menu to leave the Edit screen once you have seen your form on the screen.)
46. Sort the records stored in the SOFTWARE database in alphabetical order by the name of the software. Use SORTFLE as the filename for the sorted file.
47. After the records have been sorted, print a list of all records using Quick Report.
48. Sort the records in the database file in alphabetical order by software name within category. Use SORTFLE as the filename of the sorted file.
49. After the records have been sorted, print a list of all records using Quick Report.
50. Create an index on the Category field in the SOFTWARE database. Use it to list the records in SOFTWARE in category order.
51. Create an index on the combination of the Category and Software Name fields in the SOFTWARE database. Use it to list the records in SOFTWARE ordered by software name within category.
52. Use an index to locate the record containing image fonts.
53. Remove the index that was created on the combination of the Category and Software Name fields.
54. Design a report for data in the SOFTWARE database file. The report is to contain page and column headings. Fields to be included on the report include the Software Name, Category, Company Name, Quantity, Cost, and Total Inventory Value. The total inventory value is calculated by multiplying the cost by the quantity. A final total of the total inventory value is to be displayed.
55. Begin the report creation process for this report. Call the report SOFTRPT1. Correct the detail band.
56. Correct the report summary for SOFTRPT1.
57. Correct the page header for SOFTRPT1.
58. Print a report of all records in the SOFTWARE database file. Use the report layout stored in SOFTRPT1.
59. Print a report of those records in the SOFTWARE database file on which cost is less than $100.00. Use the report layout stored in SOFTRPT1.
60. Modify the report format stored in SOFTRPT1 so that a subtotal is taken for the total inventory value when there is a change in category. Use this report format to display all the records in the SOFTWARE database file. (**Hint**: Be sure the records are ordered correctly.)

The structure of the SOFTWARE database file is to be changed from:

SOFTWARE NAME	COMPANY	CATEGORY	MS_DOS	QUANTITY	COST
Databurst	Electric Software	Database	T	5	299.95
Type Ease	Edusoft Inc.	WP	F	22	29.95
Image Fonts	Graph Tech Inc.	WP	T	12	49.95
Data Filer	Anchor Software	Database	T	18	149.95
Master	Edusoft Inc.	Education	F	10	49.95

.
.
.

to:

SOFTWARE NAME	CATEGORY	MS_DOS	QUANTITY	COST	CMP_CODE
Databurst	Database	T	5	299.95	01
Type Ease	WP	F	22	29.95	05
Image Fonts	WP	T	12	49.95	04
Data File Manager	Database	T	18	149.95	02
Master	Education	F	10	49.95	05

.
.
.

CMP_ CODE	COMPANY NAME
01	Electric Software
02	Anchor Software
03	Learnit Software
04	Graph Tech Inc.
05	Edusoft Inc.

61. Change the length of the Software Name field in the SOFTWARE database file to accommodate "Data File Manager."

62. Add the CMP_CODE field to the SOFTWARE database.

63. Fill in the CMP_CODE field in the SOFTWARE database with the appropriate data (01 on records where the company is Electric Software, 02 on records where the company is Anchor Software, and so on).

64. Delete the Company field from the SOFTWARE database.

65. Create the new database file. Use the name SOFTCATS for this file. The CMP_CODE field should be indexed.

66. Add the indicated company codes and names to this database file.

67. Create a view called SOFTVIEW. This view should contain both the SOFTCATS and SOFTWARE database files. The CMP_CODE field in both files should be used to relate the two. Include all fields from the SOFTWARE database and the Company field from the SOFTCATS database in this view.

68. Using this view, display the software name, category, and cost for all software produced by Electric Software.

69. Using this view, display the software name, category, and cost for all software produced by Electric Software. Sort the data by category.

70. What do you think about the change that was made? Is it a good idea? What are the advantages? What are the disadvantages?

COMPREHENSIVE EXERCISE 2

You are to create a database file to store information about homes that are for sale in an area. The records contain the date the home was listed, address, city, zip code, number of bedrooms, number of bathrooms, an entry T (true) or F (false) to indicate if the home has a pool, and the selling price of the home. The homes in the database are listed in the following chart.

DATE	ADDRESS	CITY	ZIP	BDRM	BATH	POOL	PRICE
09/15/92	9661 King Pl.	Anaheim	92644	4	2	T	185000.00
09/19/92	1625 Brook St.	Fullerton	92633	3	1	F	95000.00
10/02/92	182 Oak Ave.	Fullerton	92634	4	2	T	92000.00
10/09/92	145 Oak Ave.	Garden Grove	92641	5	3	T	145000.00
10/15/92	124 Lark St.	Anaheim	92644	3	2	F	119100.00
10/22/92	926 Pine Ln.	Garden Grove	92641	3	1	F	92500.00
11/20/92	453 Adams Ave.	Costa Mesa	92688	5	3	T	185000.00
11/23/92	1456 Kern St.	Costa Mesa	92688	4	2	T	163900.00
12/10/92	862 Stanley St.	Garden Grove	92641	4	2	T	189995.00
12/13/92	1552 Weldon Pl.	Garden Grove	92641	3	2	F	169500.00

FIELD DESCRIPTION	FIELD NAME	FIELD TYPE	WIDTH	DECIMAL POSITIONS	INDEX
DATE	DATE	DATE	8		N
ADDRESS	ADDRESS	CHARACTER	16		Y
CITY	CITY	CHARACTER	12		N
ZIP	ZIP	CHARACTER	5		N
BDRM	BDRM	NUMERIC	2	0	N
BATH	BATH	NUMERIC	2	0	N
POOL	POOL	LOGICAL	1		N
PRICE	PRICE	NUMERIC	9	2	N

Perform the following tasks:

1. Insert your data disk into drive A. Then load dBASE.
2. Create a catalog called HOMESCAT.
3. Create the database file. Use the name HOMES for the database file.
4. Enter the six fields in the preceding table.
5. Enter the preceding data. When you enter the third record, enter the city as Fulerton and the price as $29000.00.
6. After you have entered the records, enter an additional record. You may make up whatever entries you wish for the fields in this record.
7. Use SHIFT-F9 to print a list of all the data.
8. Correct the third record by changing the city to Fullerton and the price to $92000.00.
9. Delete the extra record that you added. Permanently remove the record from the database file.
10. Use SHIFT-F9 to print a list of all the data.
11. Make backup copies of this database file and the corresponding production index file. Call them HOMESBCK.DBF and HOMESBCK.MDX, respectively.

12. Activate the database file so that it can be accessed.
13. Display all the fields and all the records.
14. Display the Address field, the City field, and the Price field for all records in the database.
15. Display the Price field, the Address field, the City field, and the Zip Code field for all records in the database.
16. Display the record that has 10/22/92 in the Date field.
17. Display information about the house at 145 Oak Ave.
18. Display the records for all houses listed in the city of Anaheim.
19. Display the records for all houses in the 92641 zip code area.
20. Display the records for all houses with a pool (the entry .T. in the Pool field).
21. Display the records for all houses with a price of less than $125,000.00.
22. Display the records for all houses with a price greater than $150,000.00.
23. Display the records for all houses whose address contains the word "Ave."
24. Display the records for all houses in a city that sounds like "Garten."
25. Display the records for all houses with 4 bedrooms that cost less than $100,000.00.
26. Count the number of records in the database file.
27. Find the average cost of a house in Anaheim.
28. Find the average cost of a 4-bedroom house.
29. Find the average cost of a 3-bedroom house in Garden Grove.
30. Find the average cost of houses in each city.
31. Use the "Forward search" option to find the house whose address is 1456 Kern St.
32. Use the "Forward search" option to find the first house in the HOMES database file that is in Garden Grove.
33. Use the appropriate option to locate the next house in Garden Grove.
34. Use the "Browse" option to change the price of the house at 926 Pine Ln. to $95000.00.
35. Use the "Browse" option to change the price of the house at 1456 Kern St. to $169000.00. In addition, change the number of bathrooms to 3 and the number of bedrooms to 5.
36. Use an update query to change the price of the house at 453 Adams Ave. to $190000.00.
37. Use an update query to add $2000.00 to the price of all houses in Garden Grove.
38. Use an update query to mark all houses in Costa Mesa for deletion.
39. Use an update query to unmark all houses in Costa Mesa.

40. Use the Edit screen to mark the house located at 1625 Brook St. for deletion.
41. Use the Browse screen to mark the house located at 862 Stanley St. for deletion.
42. Physically remove the marked records from the HOMES database file.
43. List all the records in the HOMES database file.
44. Create a form for the HOMES database file that is similar to the form you created for the EMPLOYEE database file. Call it HMSFORM.
45. Activate this form. Select the Edit screen to make sure the form is active. (Select the "Exit" option of the Exit menu to leave the Edit screen once you have seen your form on the screen.)
46. Sort the records stored in the HOMES database file in ascending order by price. Use SORTFLE as the filename for the sorted file.
47. After the records have been sorted, print a list of all records using Quick Report.
48. Sort the records in the database file by price within city. Use SORTFLE as the filename of the sorted file.
49. After the records have been sorted, print a list of all records using Quick Report.
50. Create an index on the City field in the HOMES database. Use it to list the records in HOMES in city order.
51. Create an index on the combination of the City and Address fields in the HOMES database. Use it to list the records in HOMES ordered by address within city.
52. Use an index to locate the record for the house at 145 Oak Ave.
53. Remove the index that was created on the combination of the City and Address fields.
54. Design a report for data in the HOMES database file. The report is to contain page and column headings. Fields to be included on the report are the Address, City, Zip Code, and Price. A final total is to be displayed of the prices of all houses. This total lists the total value of all houses for sale in an area.
55. Begin the report creation process for this report. Call the report HMSRPT1. Correct the detail band.
56. Correct the report summary for HMSRPT1.
57. Correct the page header for HMSRPT1.
58. Print a report of all records in the HOMES database file. Use the report layout stored in HMSRPT1.
59. Print a report of those records in the HOMES database file on which the price is less than $150000.00. Use the report layout stored in HMSRPT1.
60. Modify the report format stored in HMSRPT1 so that a subtotal is taken when there is a change in city. Use this report format to display all the records in the HOMES database file. (**Hint**: Be sure the records are ordered correctly.)

Max, the user of the HOMES database file, which was created in student assignment 10 of project 1, decided to make a change. Max realized that there were only a few zip codes in which the homes for sale were likely to be located. Further, since each of these zip codes uniquely identified a city, Max decided to remove the City field from the HOMES file and create a separate database file, called ZIPCODE, relating zip codes and cities. In particular, the structure is to be changed from:

DATE	ADDRESS	CITY	ZIP	BDRM	BATH	POOL	PRICE
09/15/92	9661 King Pl.	Anaheim	92644	4	2	T	185000.00
10/02/92	182 Oak Ave.	Fullerton	92634	4	2	T	92000.00
10/09/92	145 Oak Ave.	Garden Grove	92641	5	3	T	145000.00
10/15/92	124 Lark St.	Anaheim	92644	3	2	F	119000.00
10/22/92	926 Pine Ln.	Garden Grove	92641	3	1	F	92500.00

.
.
.

to:

DATE	ADDRESS	ZIP	BDRM	BATH	POOL	PRICE
09/15/92	9661 King Pl.	92644	4	2	T	185000.00
10/02/92	182 Oak Ave.	92634	4	2	T	92000.00
10/09/92	145 Oak Ave.	92641	5	3	T	145000.00
10/15/92	124 Lark St.	92644	3	2	F	119000.00
10/22/92	926 Pine Ln.	92641	3	1	F	92500.00

.
.
.

ZIP	CITY
92644	Anaheim
92641	Garden Grove
92688	Costa Mesa
92633	Fullerton
92634	Fullerton

61. Delete the City field from the HOMES database.

62. Create the new database file. Use the name ZIPCODE for this file. The Zip field should be indexed.

63. Add the indicated zip codes and cities to this database file.

64. Create a view called ZIPVIEW. This view should contain both the ZIPCODE and HOMES database files. The Zip field in both files should be used to relate the two. Include all fields from the HOMES database and the City field from the ZIPCODE database in this view.

65. Using this view, display the date, address, city, zip, and price for all homes in Fullerton.

66. Using this view, display the date, address, city, zip, and price for all homes in Fullerton. Sort the data by address.

67. What do you think about the change that was made? Is it a good idea? What are the advantages? What are the disadvantages?

Index

S

V